# Chart 5011
(INT 1 Format)
## Edition 5 - April 2011

*RAL Young*

# SYMBOLS and ABBREVIATIONS
# used on Admiralty Paper Charts

## CONTENTS

Published at Taunton, United Kingdom under the Superintendence of Rear Admiral J. A. L. Myres, FRICS, Hydrographer of the Navy, 1991.

# INTRODUCTION

*General*

Chart 5011 is primarily a key to symbols and abbreviations used on Admiralty and International paper and raster charts and leisure folios compiled by the United Kingdom Hydrographic Office (UKHO). Variations may occur on charts adopted into the Admiralty Series that were originally produced by another hydrographic office. Where these symbols and abbreviations are easily understood they will not be included as examples in this publication. Symbols and abbreviations shown on Electronic Chart Display and Information Systems (ECDIS) may differ from those described in this document.

*Schematic Layout of Chart 5011*

This edition of Chart 5011 is based on the "Chart Specifications of the IHO" (International Hydrographic Organization) adopted in 1982, with later additions and updates. The layout and numbering accords with the official IHO version of Chart INT 1 (English version produced by Germany).

① Tracks, Routes **M** ②

④ ④

| Tracks Marked by Lights → P | Leading Beacons → Q | | Tracks ③ |
|---|---|---|---|
| 1 | 2 Bns ≠ 270·5 | Leading line (the firm line is the track to be followed) | † Bn   Bn   *Bns in Line* 270°30′   Ldg Bns 270·5   270·5 | 433.1 433.2 ⑨ 433.3 |

⑤ ⑥ ⑦ ⑧

① Section.

② Section designation. (In some nautical publications, this reference is pre-fixed "I", for International.)

③ Sub-section.

④ Cross-reference to terms in other sections.

⑤ Column 1: Numbering following the International "Chart Specifications of the IHO". A letter in this column, e.g. **a**, indicates a supplementary national symbol for which there is no International equivalent.

⑥ Column 2: International (INT) symbols used on Admiralty paper charts. Where both are shown, true to scale representations are to the left of symbols.

⑦ Column 3: Term and explanation in English.

⑧ Column 4: Other symbol or abbreviation used on Admiralty paper charts, if different from Column 2.

⑨ Column 5: Not navigationally significant. Cross references to the "Chart Specifications of the IHO", S-4 (Part B, unless a reference letter to another part is given).

The mark † indicates that this representation or usage is obsolescent.
The mark # in Columns 2, 3 and 4 indicates that this symbol will only be found on paper charts adopted into the Admiralty chart series. However, users should note that on such charts additional or different symbols not listed in this publication may be used. Where not easily understood, such symbols will be explained on those charts.

**Metric Charts & Fathoms Charts**  Metric units are introduced on Admiralty charts as they are modernised (except for charts of the waters around the United States of America, where fathoms or feet continue to be used). Fathom and/or feet charts can be distinguished from metric charts by the use of grey for land areas, a note in the title block and in some cases by a prominent legend in the margin.

**Chart Datum**  On metric charts, the reference level for soundings is given under the chart title. On fathoms charts, the reference level for soundings may be given under the title; if not, it can be deduced from the tidal information panel.

**Depths**  The units used are given under the title of the chart. The position of a sounding is the centre of the area covered by the figures.

On metric charts, depths of less than 21m are generally expressed in metres and decimetres. Where source information is sufficiently precise, depths between 21m and 31m may be given in half-metres. All other depths are rounded down to whole metres.

On fathom charts, depths are generally expressed in fathoms and feet where less than 11 fms, and in fathoms elsewhere. Where source information is sufficiently precise, depths between 11 and 15 fms may be given in fathoms and feet. Older charts may show fractions of fathoms in depths of 10 fathoms or less, and some large-scale charts show all depths in feet.

On adopted or co-produced charts these ranges may vary.

**Drying heights**  Underlined figures on rocks and banks which uncover indicate heights above chart datum. They are given in metres and decimetres or in feet as appropriate.

2

| | |
|---|---|
| *Heights* | Heights are given in metres or in feet above the charted height datum; details are given in the Explanatory Notes under the chart title. The position of a height is normally that of the dot alongside it, thus ·79. Parentheses are used when the figure expressing height is set apart from the object (eg when showing the height of a small islet). Clearance heights may be referred to a higher datum than other heights. In such cases this will be stated in the Explanatory Notes. |
| *Bearings* | Bearings are given from seaward and refer to the true compass. |
| *Names* | Names on Admiralty charts are spelt in accordance with the principles and systems approved by the Permanent Committee on Geographical Names for British Official Use. |
| | A second name may be given, usually in parentheses, in the following circumstances: |
| | a. if the retention of a superseded rendering will facilitate cross-reference to related publications; |
| | b. if, in the case of a name that has changed radically, the retention of the former one will aid recognition; |
| | c. if it is decided to retain an English conventional name in addition to the present official rendering; |
| *Chart Catalogues* | Details of Admiralty charts are given in the "Catalogue of Admiralty Charts and Publications" (NP 131), and regional catalogue "North West Europe" (NP 109), both published annually. |
| *The Mariner's Handbook and other Publications* | The Mariner's Handbook (NP 100) includes information on the following: |
| | The use of charts and the degree of reliance that may be placed on them; chart supply and updating; names; charted aids to navigation; navigational hazards; traffic separation schemes; offshore oil and gas operations; tides and currents; general marine meteorology. A glossary of terms used on Admiralty charts is also given. |
| | Information about features represented on charts can also be found in the following publications or their digital equivalents: |
| | Admiralty Sailing Directions; Admiralty List of Lights and Fog Signals; Admiralty Tide Tables and Tidal Stream Atlases; Admiralty List of Radio Signals; Annual Notices to Mariners; IALA Maritime Buoyage System. |
| *How to keep your Admiralty Products up-to-date* | How to keep your Admiralty Products up-to-date (NP 294) provides comprehensive guidance on how to update both paper and digital Admiralty charts and publications. |
| *Copyright* | Admiralty charts and publications (including this one) are protected by Crown Copyright. They are derived from Crown Copyright information and from copyright information published by other organisations. They may not be reproduced in any material form (including photocopying or storing by electronic means) without prior permission of the copyright owners, which may be sought by applying, in the first instance, to the Copyright Manager; The United Kingdom Hydrographic Office, Admiralty Way, Taunton, Somerset TA1 2DN, UK. |

*Schematic Layout of an Admiralty INT chart (reduced in size)*

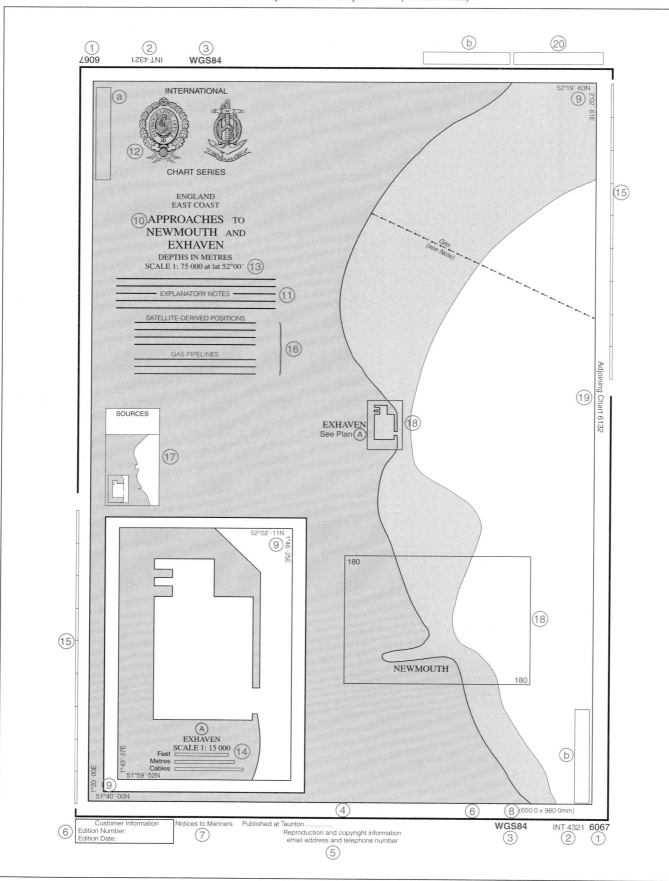

# Chart Number, Title, Marginal Notes  **A**

*Magnetic Features* → B          *Tidal Data* → H          *Satellite Navigation Systems* → S

(1)  *Chart number in the Admiralty series.*                                                                                     251

(2)  *Chart number in the International (INT) Chart series.*                                                                      251.1

(3)  *Use of WGS84 geodetic reference system. A reference to the depth units may be shown*                                        201
                                                                                                                                 255

(4)  *Publication note (imprint) showing the date of publication as a New Chart.*                                                 252.1
                                                                                                                                 252.4

(5)  *Reproduction and Copyright acknowledgement note. All Admiralty charts are subject to Crown Copyright restrictions.*         253

(6)  *Customer Information, Edition Number, Edition Date, (charts revised prior to May 2000 have New Edition date at bottom right of chart)*   252.2

(7)  *Notices to Mariners: (a) the year dates and numbers of Notices to Mariners and (b) the dates (usually bracketed) of minor updates included in reprints but not formally promulgated (abandoned as a method of updating in 1986), (charts revised prior to May 2000 have the legend 'Small corrections').*   252.3

(8)  *Dimensions of the inner neat-lines of the chart border. In the case of charts on Transverse Mercator and Gnomonic projections, dimensions may be quoted for all borders of the chart which differ. Some Fathoms charts show the dimensions in inches e.g. (38.40 x 25.40).*   222.3
                                                                                                                                 222.4

(9)  *Corner co-ordinates.*                                                                                                       214

(10) *Chart title. This should be quoted, in addition to the chart number, when ordering a chart.*                               241.3

(11) *Explanatory notes on chart content;* **to be read before using the chart**.                                                242

(12) *Seals. Where an Admiralty chart is in the International Chart series, the seal of the International Hydrographic Organization (IHO) is shown in addition to the national seal. Reproductions of international charts of other nations (facsimile) have the seals of the original producer (left), publisher (centre) and the IHO (right). Reproductions of other charts have the seals of original producer (left) and publisher (right); charts which are co-productions carry the seals of the nations involved in their production.*   241.1
                                                                                                                                 241.2

(13) *Scale of chart; on Mercator projection, at a stated latitude.*                                                             211
                                                                                                                                 241.4

(14) *Linear scales on large-scale plan.*                                                                                         221

(15) *Linear border scales (metres). On smaller scale charts, the latitude border should be used to measure Sea Miles and Cables.*   221.1

(16) *Cautionary notes (if any) on charted detail;* **to be read before using the chart**.                                       242

(17) *Source Diagram (if any). If a Source Diagram is not shown, details of the sources used in the compilation of the chart are given in the explanatory notes (see 11).* **The Source Diagram or notes should be studied carefully before using the chart in order to assess the reliability of the sources**.   290-298

(18) *Reference to a larger scale chart or plan (with reference letter if plan on same chart).*                                   254

(19) *Reference to an adjoining chart of similar scale.*                                                                          254

(20) *Note* 'IMPORTANT - THE USE OF ADMIRALTY CHARTS'.                                                                           243

(a)  *Conversion scales. To allow approximate conversions between metric and fathoms and feet units. On older charts, conversion tables are given instead.*   280

(b)  *Copyright Notice*

# B Positions, Distances, Directions, Compass

| Geographical Positions | | | | | |
|---|---|---|---|---|---|
| 1 | Lat | *Latitude* | | | |
| 2 | Long | *Longitude* | | | |
| 3 | | *International Meridian (Greenwich)* | | | |
| 4 | ° | *Degree(s)* | | | 130 |
| 5 | ′ | *Minute(s) of arc* | | | 130 |
| 6 | ″ | *Second(s) of arc* | | | 130 |
| 7 | *PA* | *Position approximate (not accurately determined or does not remain fixed)* | † (PA) | † (P.A.) | 417<br>424.1 |
| 8 | *PD* | *Position doubtful (reported in various positions)* | † (PD) | † (P.D.) | 417<br>424.2 |
| 9 | N | *North* | | | 131.1 |
| 10 | E | *East* | | | 131.1 |
| 11 | S | *South* | | | 131.1 |
| 12 | W | *West* | | | 131.1 |
| 13 | NE | *North-east* | | | |
| 14 | SE | *South-east* | | | |
| 15 | NW | *North-west* | | | |
| 16 | SW | *South-west* | | | |

| Control Points, Distance Marks | | | | | |
|---|---|---|---|---|---|
| 20 | △ | *Triangulation point* | | | 304.1 |
| 21 | ⊕ | *Observation spot* | † + Obs Spot | † + *Obsn. Spot* | 304.2 |
| 22 | ⊙ ⊙ | *Fixed point* | | | 305.1<br>340.5 |
| 23 | ⊼ | *Benchmark* | † ⊼ BM | † ⊼ B.M. | 304.3 |
| 24 | | *Boundary mark* | | | 306 |
| 25.1 | ○ *km 32* | *Distance along waterway, no visible marker* | | | 307<br>361.3 |
| 25.2 | ○ km 32 | *Distance along waterway, with visible marker* | | | |
| a | | *Viewpoint* | ○ See View | | 390.2 |

| Symbolised Positions (Examples) | | | | | |
|---|---|---|---|---|---|
| 30 | # $18_3$ Wk | *Symbols in plan: position is centre of primary symbol* | | | 305.1 |
| 31 | | *Symbols in profile: position is at bottom of symbol* | | | 305.1 |
| 32 | ⊙ Mast ⊙ MAST ☆ | *Point symbols (accurate positions)* | | | 305.1<br>340.5 |
| 33 | ○ Mast PA | *Approximate position* | † ⊙ Mast PA | | 305.1 |

| | | | Units | |
|---|---|---|---|---|
| | | | | Units |
| 40 | km | Kilometre(s) | | |
| 41 | m | Metre(s) | | 130 |
| 42 | dm | Decimetre(s) | | 130 |
| 43 | cm | Centimetre(s) | | |
| 44 | mm | Millimetre(s) | | 130 |
| 45 | M | International Nautical Mile(s) (1852m) or Sea Mile(s) | n mile(s) M | 130 |
| 46 | | Cable (0.1M) | | 130 |
| 47 | ft | Foot/feet | | |
| 48 | | Fathom(s) | fm., fms. | |
| 49 | h | Hour | | 130 |
| 50 | # m / min | Minute(s) of time | | 130 |
| 51 | s / # sec | Second(s) of time | † sec | 130 |
| 52 | kn | Knot(s) | | 130 |
| 53 | t | Tonne(s), Ton(s), tonnage (weight) | | 328.3 |
| 54 | # cd | Candela | | |

| | | | Magnetic Compass | |
|---|---|---|---|---|
| | | | | Magnetic Compass |
| 60 | | Variation | Var | |
| 61 | | Magnetic | Mag | |
| 62 | | Bearing | | 132 |
| 63 | | true | | |
| 64 | | decreasing | decrg | |
| 65 | | increasing | incrg | |
| 66 | | Annual change | | |
| 67 | | Deviation | | |
| 68.1 | # Magnetic Variation 4°30´W 2010 (8´E) | Note of magnetic variation, in position | | 272.2 |
| 68.2 | # Magnetic Variation at 55°N 8°W 4°30´W 2010 (8´E) | Note of magnetic variation, out of position | Magnetic Variation: 4°30´W 2010 (10´E) | |

# B Positions, Distances, Directions, Compass

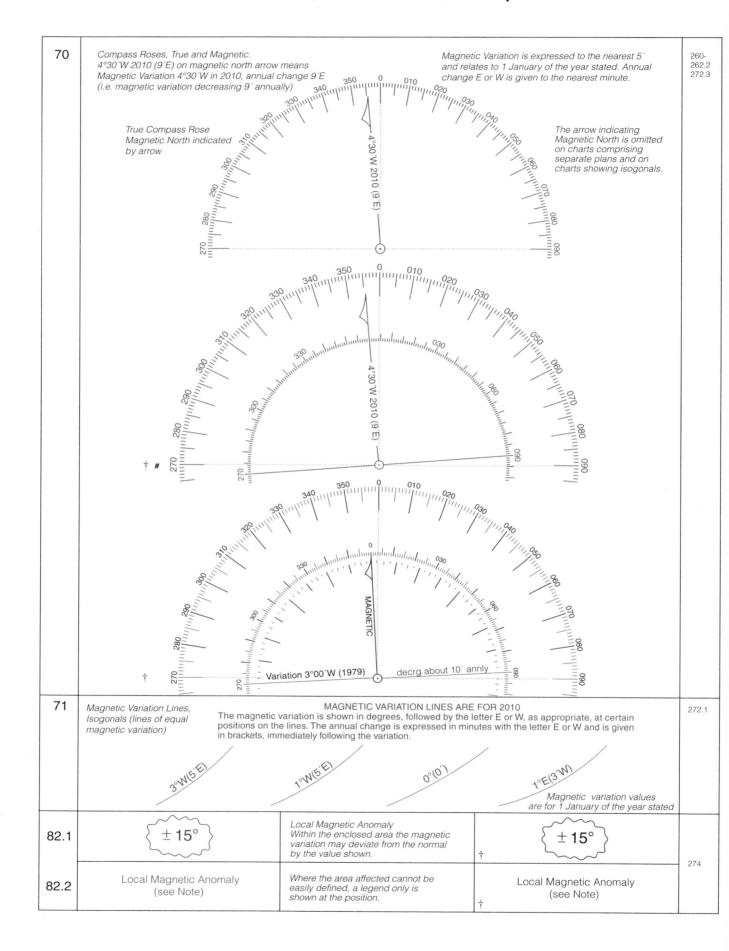

| 70 | Compass Roses, True and Magnetic.<br>4°30´W 2010 (9´E) on magnetic north arrow means<br>Magnetic Variation 4°30´W in 2010, annual change 9´E<br>(i.e. magnetic variation decreasing 9´ annually) | Magnetic Variation is expressed to the nearest 5´<br>and relates to 1 January of the year stated. Annual<br>change E or W is given to the nearest minute. | 260-<br>262.2<br>272.3 |

*True Compass Rose Magnetic North indicated by arrow*

4°30´W 2010 (9´E)

*The arrow indicating Magnetic North is omitted on charts comprising separate plans and on charts showing isogonals.*

† #  4°30´W 2010 (9´E)

† MAGNETIC  Variation 3°00´W (1979)  decrg about 10´ annly

| 71 | *Magnetic Variation Lines,*<br>*Isogonals (lines of equal*<br>*magnetic variation)* | MAGNETIC VARIATION LINES ARE FOR 2010<br>The magnetic variation is shown in degrees, followed by the letter E or W, as appropriate, at certain<br>positions on the lines. The annual change is expressed in minutes with the letter E or W and is given<br>in brackets, immediately following the variation. | 272.1 |

3°W(5´E)    1°W(5´E)    0°(0´)    1°E(3´W)

*Magnetic variation values are for 1 January of the year stated*

| 82.1 | ±15° | Local Magnetic Anomaly<br>Within the enclosed area the magnetic<br>variation may deviate from the normal<br>by the value shown. | ±15° | |
| 82.2 | Local Magnetic Anomaly<br>(see Note) | Where the area affected cannot be<br>easily defined, a legend only is<br>shown at the position. | Local Magnetic Anomaly<br>(see Note) | 274 |

| | | | | |
|---|---|---|---|---|
| *Foreshore → I, J* | | | | Coastline |
| 1 | | Coastline, surveyed | | 310.1<br>310.2 |
| 2 | | Coastline, unsurveyed | | 311 |
| 3 | | Steep coast, Cliffs | | 312.1 |
| 4 | | Hillocks | | 312.1 |
| 5 | | Flat coast | | 312.2 |
| 6 | | Sandy shore | | 312.2 |
| 7 | | Stony shore, Shingly shore | | 312.2 |
| 8 | | Sandhills, Dunes | | 312.3 |

| | | | | |
|---|---|---|---|---|
| *Plane of Reference for Heights → H* | | | | Relief |
| 10 | | Contour lines with values and spot height | | 351.3<br>351.4<br>351.5<br>351.6<br>352.2 |
| 11 | | Spot heights | | 352.1<br>352.2 |
| 12 | | Approximate contour lines with values and approximate height | | 351.3<br>351.4<br>351.5<br>351.6<br>352.3 |

# C  Natural Features

| | | | | |
|---|---|---|---|---|
| 13 | | *Form lines with spot height* | | 351.2<br>351.3<br>351.7<br>352.2 |
| 14 | | *Approximate height of top of trees (above height datum)* | | 352.4 |

| Water Features, Lava | | | | |
|---|---|---|---|---|
| 20 | | *River, Stream* | | 353.1<br>353.2<br>353.4 |
| 21 | | *Intermittent river* | | 353.3 |
| 22 | | *Rapids, Waterfalls* | | 353.5 |
| 23 | | *Lakes* | | 353.6 |
| 24 | | *Salt pans* | | 353.7 |
| 25 | | *Glacier* | | 353.8 |
| 26 | | *Lava flow* | | 355 |

10

| | | | Vegetation | |
|---|---|---|---|---|
| 30 | Wooded | Woods in general | | 354.1 |
| 31 | | Prominent trees (isolated or in groups) | | 354.2 |
| 31.1 | | Deciduous tree, unknown or unspecified tree | | |
| 31.2 | | Evergreen (except conifer) | | |
| 31.3 | | Conifer | | |
| 31.4 | | Palm | | |
| 31.5 | | Nipa palm | | |
| 31.6 | | Casuarina | | |
| 31.7 | | Filao | | |
| 31.8 | | Eucalypt | | |
| 32 | | Mangrove | | 312.4 |
| 33 | Marsh  Marsh | Marsh, Swamp, Salt marsh, Reed beds | Saltings   Saltings | 312.2 |

# D Cultural Features

## Settlements, Buildings

Height of objects → E          Landmarks → E

| No. | | | Description | | No. ref |
|---|---|---|---|---|---|
| 1 | | | Urban area | | 370.3 370.4 |
| 2 | | | Settlement with scattered buildings | | 370.5 |
| 3 | ○ Name | ▭ Name # | Settlement (on medium and small-scale charts) | ■ Name | 370.7 |
| 4 | ⊹ Name | ■ Name HOTEL | Inland village | | 370.6 |
| 5 | ▬  ⌐  ▭  ▬  ▭ | | Building | Bldg | 370.5 |
| 6 | ■ Name  Hotel | ■ Name  Hotel | Important building in built-up area | | 370.3 |
| 7 | NAME | NAME | Street name, Road name | | 371 |
| 8 | Ru | ⛫ Ru | Ruin, Ruined landmark | † ⛫ (ru) | 378 378.2 |

## Roads, Railways, Airfields

| No. | | | Description | | No. ref |
|---|---|---|---|---|---|
| 10 | | | Motorway | | 365.1 |
| 11 | | | Road (hard surfaced) | | 365.2 |
| 12 | | | Track, Path (loose or unsurfaced) | | 365.3 |
| 13 | # | # | Railway, with station | † Rly  † Ry  † Sta  † Stn | 328.4 362.1 362.2 |
| 14 | | | Cutting | † ⬭  † ⬭ | 363.2 |
| 15 | | | Embankment | † ⬭  † ⬭ | 364.1 |
| 16 | | | Tunnel | | 363.1 |
| 17 | | Airfield  ✈  Airport | Airport, Airfield | | 366.1 366.2 |
| a | | | Tramway | | |
| b | | | Helicopter landing site, Heliport | Ⓗ | |

| | Plane of Reference for Heights → H | | | Other Cultural Features | | |
|---|---|---|---|---|---|---|
| 20 | | | Vertical clearance above Height Datum (in parentheses when displaced for clarity) | (17)† (H 17m)† | (Headway 55ft)† | 380.1 380.2 |
| 21 | | | Horizontal clearance | | | 380.3 |
| 22 | | | Fixed bridge with vertical clearance | (20)† | | 381.1 |
| 23.1 | | | Opening bridge (in general) with vertical clearance | † (20) | | 381.3 |
| 23.2 | Swing Bridge | | Swing bridge with vertical clearance | | | |
| 23.3 | Lifting Bridge (open 12) | | Lifting bridge with vertical clearance (closed and open) | | | |
| 23.4 | Bascule Bridge | | Bascule bridge with vertical clearance | | | |
| 23.5 | Pontoon Bridge | | Pontoon bridge | † | | |
| 23.6 | Draw Bridge | | Draw bridge with vertical clearance | | | |
| 24 | Transporter Bridge | | Transporter bridge with vertical clearance between Height Datum and lowest part of structure | | | 381.2 |
| 25 | | | Overhead transporter, Aerial cableway with vertical clearance | † Transporter (7) | | 382.3 |
| 26 | Pyl ⦃28⦄ Pyl | | Overhead power cable with pylons and safe vertical clearance (see **Note** below D29) | † Power (H 30m) Power Overhead (H.98ft) | | 382.1 |
| 27 | | | Overhead cable, Telephone line, with vertical clearance | † H 20m Overhead (H.64ft) | | 382 382.2 |
| 28 | Overhead pipe | | Overhead pipe with vertical clearance | | | 383 |
| 29 | | | Pipeline on land | † Pipeline | | 377 |

**Note**: The safe vertical clearance above Height Datum, as defined by the responsible authority, is given in magenta where known (see H20); otherwise the physical vertical clearance is shown in black as in D20.

# E Landmarks

| General | Plane of Reference for Heights → H | | Lighthouses → P | Beacons → Q | |
|---|---|---|---|---|---|
| 1 | ◆ Factory   ⊙ Hotel   ☖ | Examples of landmarks | | | 340.1<br>340.2<br>340.5 |
| 2 | ◆ FACTORY   ⊙ HOTEL   ☖ WATER TOWER | Examples of conspicuous landmarks. A legend in capital letters indicates that a feature is conspicuous | | † | conspic | 340.1<br>340.2<br>340.3<br>340.5 |
| 3.1 | | Pictorial sketches (in true position) | | | 340.7<br>373.1<br>390<br>456.5<br>457.3 |
| 3.2 | | Pictorial sketches (out of position) | | | |
| 4 | ☖ (30) | Height of top of a structure above height datum | | | 302.3 |
| 5 | ☖ (30̄) | Height of top of a structure above ground level | | | 303 |

## Landmarks

| 10.1 | ⊕   ✠ | Ch | Church, Cathedral | | † | Cath | 373.1<br>373.2 |
|---|---|---|---|---|---|---|---|
| 10.2 | ⊕ Tr   ✠ Tr | | Church tower | | | | 373.2 |
| 10.3 | ⊕ Sp   ✠ Sp | | Church spire | | | | 373.2 |
| 10.4 | ⊕ Cup   ✠ Cup | | Church cupola | | | | 373.2 |
| 11 | | | Chapel | | ✠ | Ch | |
| 12 | | | Cross, Calvary | | # | † | |
| 13 | ⋈ | | Temple | | † | ⊞ | 373.3 |
| 14 | ⋈ | | Pagoda | | | Pag | 373.3 |
| 15 | ⋈ | | Shinto shrine, Joss house | | | | 373.3 |
| 16 | ⋈   卍# | | Buddhist temple or shrine | | † | 卍 | 373.3 |
| 17 | ☽ | | Mosque, Minaret | | † | ☪ | 373.4 |
| 18 | # ⊙ Marabout | | Marabout | | ⊙ Tomb | † ☽ | 373.5 |
| 19 | Cemetery (all religions symbol) | | Cemetery (all religions) | | † | ††† Cemy | 373.6 |
| 20 | ☖ | Tr | Tower | | | | 374.3 |
| 21 | ☖ | | Water tower, Water tank on a tower | | ⊙ Water Tr | | 374.2<br>376 |

| | | | | | | | |
|---|---|---|---|---|---|---|---|
| 22 | ⌠ | ◣ Chy | Chimney | | | | 374.1 |
| 23 | ◊ | | Flare stack (on land) | | | | 374.1 |
| 24 | ⌠ | Mon | Monument (including column, pillar, obelisk, statue) | † Mont | | † Col | 374.4 |
| 25.1 | ✕ | | Windmill | | | | 374.5 |
| 25.2 | ✕ Ru | | Windmill (without sails) | † ✕ (ru) | | | 378.2 |
| 26.1 | ⌠ | Wind turbine / Windmotor | Wind turbine | † ⌠ | | † ✿ | 374.6 |
| 26.2 | ⌠ | ⌠ | Wind farm | | | | 374.6 |
| 27 | ⌐ | FS | Flagstaff, Flagpole | | | | 374.7 |
| 28 | ⌠ | | Radio mast, Television mast, Mast | ⊙ Radio mast / ⊙ TV mast | | ⌠ | 375.1 |
| 29 | ⌠ | | Radio tower, Television tower | ⊙ Radio Tr / ⊙ TV Tr | | | 375.2 |
| 30.1 | ⊙ Radar Mast | ⌠ Radar | Radar mast | | | | |
| 30.2 | ⊙ Radar Tr | ⌠ Radar | Radar tower | ⌠ | | | 487.3 |
| 30.3 | ⊙ Radar Sc | | Radar scanner | ⌠ | | | |
| 30.4 | ⊙ Radome | | Radome | | | | |
| 31 | ⌠ | | Dish aerial | † ⊙ Dish aerial | | | 375.4 |
| 32 | ▦ ⊕ • | Tanks | Tanks | † ○ | | | 376.1 376.2 |
| 33 | ○ Silo | ⊙ Silo | Silo | | | | 376.3 |
| 34.1 | ◿ Fort | | Fortified structure (on large-scale charts) | | | | 379.1 |
| 34.2 | ⊡ | | Castle, Fort, Blockhouse (on smaller scale charts) | † ⟡ Ft | | Cas | 379.2 |
| 34.3 | ⊡ | | Battery, Small fort (on smaller scale charts) | † ⌣ Batt | | Baty | 379.2 |
| 35.1 | ⏖ | | Quarry (on large-scale charts) | † ⛏ | | | 367.1 |
| 35.2 | ✗ | | Quarry (on smaller scale charts) | | | | 367.2 |
| 36 | ✗ | | Mine | | | | 367.2 |
| 37.1 | ⊞ | | Caravan site | | | | |
| | # | | | | | | 368 |
| 37.2 | △ | | Camping site, camping and caravan site | | | | |

# F Ports

| | | | Protection Structures | | | |
|---|---|---|---|---|---|---|
| **Protection Structures** | | | | | | |
| 1 | | | Dyke, Levee, Berm | | | 313.1 |
| 2.1 | | | Seawall (on large-scale charts) | | | 313.2 |
| 2.2 | | | Seawall (on smaller scale charts) | | | |
| 3 | Causeway | | Causeway | | | 313.3 |
| 4.1 | | | Breakwater (in general) | | | 322.1 |
| 4.2 | | | Breakwater (loose boulders, tetrapods, etc) | (covers) | | |
| 4.3 | | | Breakwater (slope of concrete or masonry) | | | |
| 5 | Training Wall (covers) Training Wall Training Wall (covers) Training Bank (covers) | | Training wall | | | 322.2 |
| 6.1 | | | Groyne (always dry) | | | 313.4 324 |
| 6.2 | | | Groyne (intertidal) | | | |
| 6.3 | | | Groyne (always underwater) | | | |

| Harbour Installations | Depths → I | Anchorages, Limits → N | Beacons and other fixed marks → Q | Marina → U | | |
|---|---|---|---|---|---|---|
| 10 | 🐟 | | Fishing harbour | | | 320.1 |
| 11.1 | ⚓ | | Boat Harbour, Marina | | | |
| 11.2 | ⛵ | | Yacht berth without facilities | | | 320.2 |
| 11.3 | ▶ | | Yacht club, Sailing club | | | |

| | | | | |
|---|---|---|---|---|
| 12 | | Mole (with berthing facility) | | 321.3 |
| 13 | | Quay, Wharf | Whf | 321.1 |
| 14 | Pier | Pier, Jetty | | 321.2 321.4 |
| 15 | Promenade Pier | Promenade pier | | 321.2 |
| 16 | Pontoon | Pontoon | | 326.9 |
| 17 | Lndg / Lndg | Landing for boats | † Ldg | 324.2 |
| 18 | | Steps, Landing stairs | | |
| 19.1 | ④ B 234 | Designation of berth | † ④ | 323.1 |
| 19.2 | Ⓥ | Visitors' berth | | 323.2 |
| 20 | ⬡ □ Dn Dns | Dolphin | | 327.1 |
| 21 | ⚓ | Deviation dolphin | | 327.2 |
| 22 | • | Minor post or pile | | 327.3 |
| 23 | Slip | Slipway, Patent slip, Ramp | | 324.1 |
| 24 | | Gridiron, Scrubbing grid | | 326.8 |
| 25 | | Dry dock, Graving dock | † | 326.1 |
| 26 | Floating Dock | Floating dock | † † † | 326.2 |
| 27 | 7·6m | Non-tidal basin, Wet dock | | 326.3 |
| 28 | | Tidal basin, Tidal harbour | | 326.4 |
| 29.1 | Floating Barrier | Floating barrier | | 449.2 |
| 29.2 | | Oil retention barrier (high pressure pipe) | | |

# F  Ports

| | | | | | | | |
|---|---|---|---|---|---|---|---|
| 30 | Dock under construction (2011) | Works on land, with year date | | | | | 329.1 |
| 31 | Being reclaimed (2011) | Works at sea, Area under reclamation, with year date | | | | | 329.2 |
| 32 | Under construction (2011)  Works in progress (2011) | Works under construction, with year date | const | † constrn. | † constn | | 329  329.4 |
| 33.1 | Ru | Ruin | | | | | 378.1 |
| 33.2 | Pier (ru) | Ruined pier, partly submerged at high water | | | | | |
| 34 | Hulk    Hulk | Hulk | | | | | |
| a | | Bollard | | ∘ Bol | | | |

| Rivers, Canals, Barrages | | *Clearances* → D | *Signal Stations* → T | *Cultural Features* → D | |
|---|---|---|---|---|---|
| 40 | | Canal | | | 361.6 |
| 41.1 | Lock | Lock (on large-scale charts) | | | 326.6  361.6 |
| 41.2 | ≪    ≪ | Lock (on smaller scale charts) | † ← | | |
| 42 | | Caisson, Gate | | | 326.5 |
| 43 | Flood Barrage | Flood barrage | | | 326.7 |
| 44 | Dam    F F | Dam, Weir  → Direction of flow | | | 364.2 |

| Transhipment Facilities | | *Roads* → D | *Railways* → D | *Tanks* → E | |
|---|---|---|---|---|---|
| 50 | RoRo | Roll-on, Roll-off (RoRo) Ferry Terminal | | | 321.5 |
| 51 | 2  3    2  3 | Transit shed, Warehouse (with designation) | | | 328.1 |
| 52 | ♯ | Timber yard | | | 328.2 |
| 53.1 | (3t) | Crane (with lifting capacity)  Travelling crane on railway | | | 328.3 |
| 53.2 | (50t) | Container crane (with lifting capacity) | | | |
| 53.3 | ⊙ SHEERLEGS | Sheerlegs (conspicuous) | | | |

| Public Buildings | | | | |
|---|---|---|---|---|
| 60 | ⚓ | Harbour Master's office | † Hr Mr | 325.1 |
| 61 | ⊖ | Custom office | | 325.2 |
| 62.1 | ⊕ | Health office, Quarantine building | | 325.3 |
| 62.2 | ⊕ Hospital | Hospital | ⊕ Hosp    † Hospl | |
| 63 | † ✉ | Post office | † PO | 372.1 |

# H  Tides, Currents

| Terms Relating to Tidal Levels | | | | |
|---|---|---|---|---|
| 1 | CD | *Chart Datum*<br>*Datum for sounding reduction* | | 405 |
| 2 | LAT | *Lowest Astronomical Tide* | | 405.3 |
| 3 | HAT | *Highest Astronomical Tide* | | |
| 4 | MLW | *Mean Low Water* | | |
| 5 | MHW | *Mean High Water* | | |
| 6 | MSL | *Mean Sea Level* | | |
| 7 | | *Land survey datum* | | |
| 8 | MLWS | *Mean Low Water Springs* | | |
| 9 | MHWS | *Mean High Water Springs* | | |
| 10 | MLWN | *Mean Low Water Neaps* | | |
| 11 | MHWN | *Mean High Water Neaps* | | |
| 12 | MLLW | *Mean Lower Low Water* | | |
| 13 | MHHW | *Mean Higher High Water* | | |
| 14 | MHLW | *Mean Higher Low Water* | | |
| 15 | MLHW | *Mean Lower High Water* | | |
| 16 | Sp | *Spring tide* | † Spr. | |
| 17 | Np | *Neap tide* | | |
| a | | *High Water* | HW | |
| b | | *Low Water* | LW | |
| c | | *Mean Tide Level* | MTL | |
| d | | *Ordnance Datum* | OD | |

20

*Vertical clearance* → D          *Tide Gauge* → T          Tidal Levels and Charted Data

**20**  *NOTE: Planes of reference are not exactly as shown below for all charts. They are usually defined in notes under chart titles.*

302.2
380.1
405

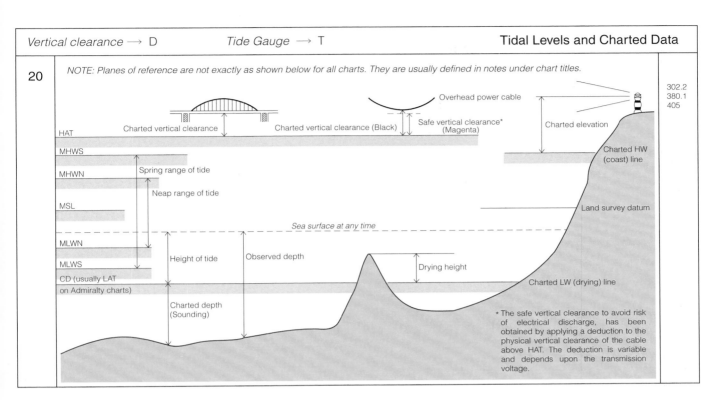

* The safe vertical clearance to avoid risk of electrical discharge, has been obtained by applying a deduction to the physical vertical clearance of the cable above HAT. The deduction is variable and depends upon the transmission voltage.

---

Tide Tables

**30**  *Tabular statement of semi-diurnal or diurnal tides*

406.2
406.3
406.4
406.5

Tidal Levels referred to Datum of Soundings

| Place | Lat. N/S | Long. E/W | Heights in metres/feet above datum | | | | Datum and Remarks |
|---|---|---|---|---|---|---|---|
| | | | MHWS | MHWN | MLWN | MLWS | |
| | | | | | | | |
| | | | MHHW | MLHW | MHLW | MLLW | |
| | | | | | | | |

**31**  *Tidal stream table*

407.2
407.3

Tidal streams referred to....

| Hours | ◇ Geographical Position | | | ◈A | ◈B | ◈C | ◈D | ◈E |
|---|---|---|---|---|---|---|---|---|
| | Directions of streams (degrees) | Rates at spring tides (knots) | Rates at neap tides (knots) | | | | | |

Before High Water: 6, 5, 4, 3, 2, 1
High Water
After High Water: 1, 2, 3, 4, 5, 6

-6, -5, -4, -3, -2, -1, 0, +1, +2, +3, +4, +5, +6

E: No

Maximum Rates

For predictions, use Admiralty Tide Tables

# H Tides, Currents

| | Tidal Streams and Currents | | | |
|---|---|---|---|---|
| 40 | →3kn→ | Flood tide stream (with mean spring rate) | † →•→  The number of black dots on the tidal stream arrows indicates the number of hours after High or Low Water at which the streams are running | 407.4 408.2 |
| 41 | →2, 8kn→ | Ebb tide stream (with mean spring rate) | † →•→ | 407.4 408.2 |
| 42 | # »»»→  ∿∿∿→ | Current in restricted waters | † »»»→ | 408.2 |
| 43 | ∿∿∿→ (see Note) | Ocean current. Details of current strength and seasonal variations may be shown | | 408.3 |
| 44 | ∿∿∿  ∿∿∿  ∿∿∿  ∿∿∿ | Overfalls, tide rips, races | † ≋ | 423.1 |
| 45 | ◎ ◎ ◎ ◎ ◎ ◎ ◎ ◎ | Eddies | | 423.3 |
| 46 | ◇D◇ | Position of tabulated tidal stream data with designation | † ◇D◇ | 407.2 |
| 47 | [a] | Offshore position for which tidal levels are tabulated | | 406.5 |
| e | | Wave recorder | † ⊙ Wave recorder | |
| f | | Current meter | † ⊙ Current meter | |

22

| | | | | |
|---|---|---|---|---|
| | | | | **General** |
| 1 | ED | Existence doubtful | † (ED) | 417 424.3 |
| 2 | SD | Sounding of doubtful depth | | 417 424.4 |
| 3.1 | Rep | Reported, but not confirmed | † Repd | 417 424.5 |
| 3.2 | Rep (1973) | Reported, with year of report, but not confirmed | † Repd (1973) | |
| 4 | :184: · · :212: | Reported, but not confirmed, sounding or danger (on small-scale charts only) | | S-4 Part C 404.3 |
| a | | Unexamined | unexam † unexamd | |

| | *Plane of Reference for Depths → H* | *Plane of Reference for Heights → H* | **Soundings and Drying Heights** | |
|---|---|---|---|---|
| 10 | 12　　9₂　　# 9,7 | Sounding in true position | | 403.1 410/412 412.1 |
| 11 | ·(4₈)　+ (12)　⊙ 3349 | Alongside depth, Sounding out of position | ·(8₃) (10₄)　# +1₈ ₈7 7₁ | 412 412.1 412.2 |
| 12 | }(14₇) | Least depth in narrow channel | | 412 412.1 412.2 |
| 13 | 330 (dotted underline/overline) | No bottom found at depth shown | | 412.3 |
| 14 | 12　　9₁ | Soundings which are unreliable (eg: taken from old or smaller scale sources) shown in upright, hairline figures | | 412.4 417.3 |
| 15 | 4₉ 4 0₉ 2 3₄ 2 0 | Drying heights and contours above chart datum | | 413 413.1 413.2 |
| 16 | 1₄ 0 2₅ 0₆ 1₇ 2₇ | Natural watercourse (in intertidal area) | | 413.3 |

| | *Plane of Reference for Depths → H* | | **Depths in Fairways and Areas** | |
|---|---|---|---|---|
| 20 | - - - - - - - - - - - - - - - - - - | Limit of dredged channel or area (major and minor) | # ——————————— | 414.3 |
| 21 | 7·0m　3·5m | Dredged channel or area with depth of dredging in metres and decimetres | Depths may be shown as **3,5** or **3**₅ on some adopted charts | 414 |
| 22 | 17m (2011)　Dredged to 8·2m (2011) | Dredged channel or area with depth of dredging and year of the latest control survey | | 414.1 |
| 23 | 17·0m　Maintained depth 13·5m | Dredged channel or area with depth regularly maintained | | 414.2 |

# I Depths

| | | | | |
|---|---|---|---|---|
| 24 | 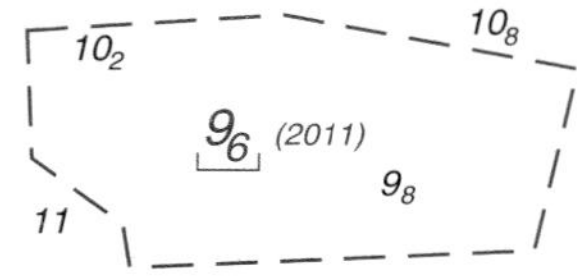 10₂ 10₈ 9₆ (2011) 9₈ 11 | *Area swept by wire drag. The depth is shown at Chart Datum. (The latest date of sweeping may be shown in parentheses)* | 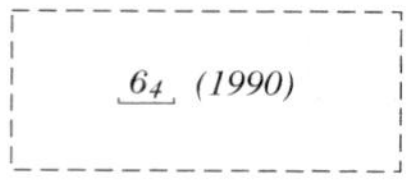 6₄ (1990) † | 415<br>415.1 |
| 25 |  Unsurveyed 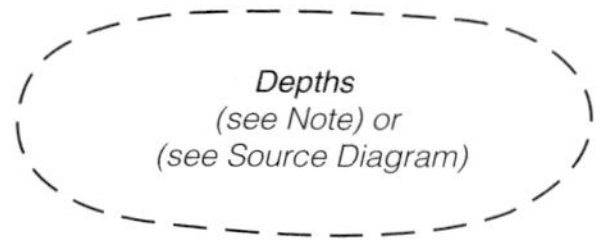 Depths<br>(see Note) or<br>(see Source Diagram) # 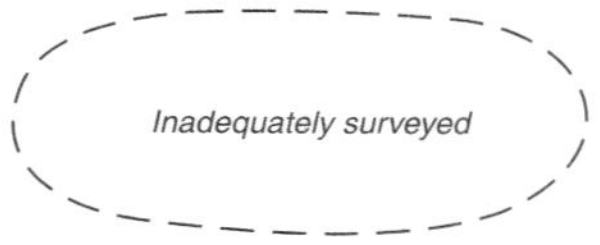 Inadequately surveyed # 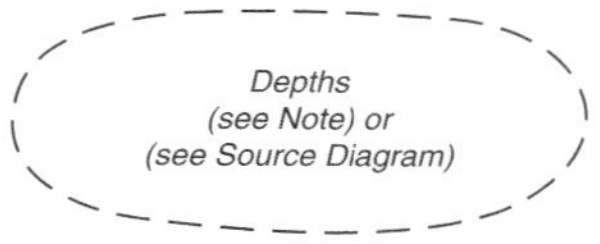 Depths<br>(see Note) or<br>(see Source Diagram) # 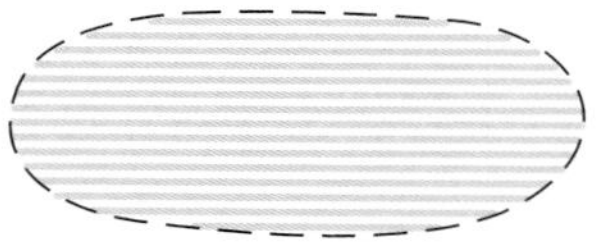 | *Unsurveyed or inadequately surveyed area; area with inadequate depth information* | | 410<br>417<br>417.6<br>417.7<br>418 |

## Depth Contours

| | | | | |
|---|---|---|---|---|
| 30 | 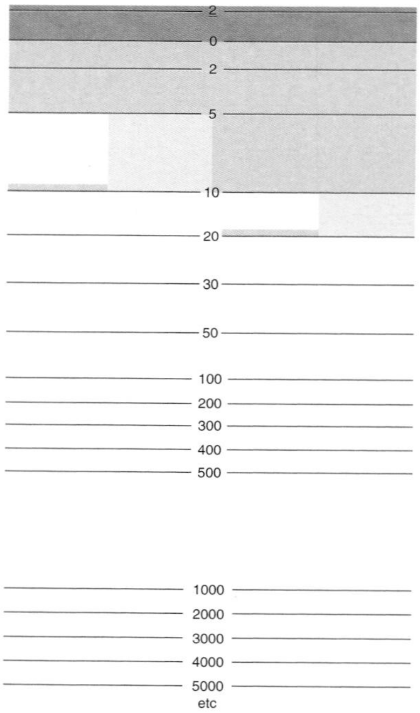 2<br>0<br>2<br>5<br>10<br>20<br>30<br>50<br>100<br>200<br>300<br>400<br>500<br>1000<br>2000<br>3000<br>4000<br>5000<br>etc | *Dries 2m contour*<br>*Low Water (LW) Line, Drying Line, Chart Datum (CD)*<br><br>*Blue tint, in one or more shades, and tint ribbons, are shown to different limits according to the scale and purpose of the chart and the nature of the bathymetry.*<br><br>*On some charts, the standard set of contours is augmented by additional contours in order to delimit particular bathymetric features or for the benefit of particular categories of shipping. However, in some instances where the provision of additional contours would be helpful, the survey data available does not permit it.*<br><br>*On some charts, contours are printed in blue.* | *On charts showing depths in fathoms/feet, the following contours are used:*<br>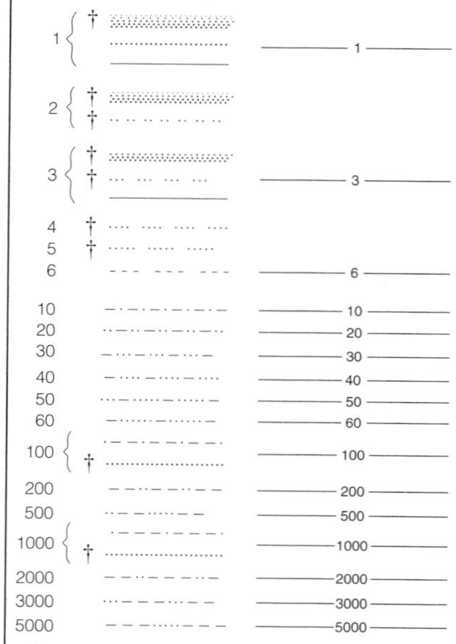 1 † 1<br>2 † †<br>3 † † 3<br>4 †<br>5 †<br>6 6<br>10 10<br>20 20<br>30 30<br>40 40<br>50 50<br>60 60<br>100 † 100<br>200 200<br>500 500<br>1000 † 1000<br>2000 2000<br>3000 3000<br>5000 5000<br>*On some recently-corrected charts, contours may be shown by continuous lines.* | 404.2<br>410<br>411 |
| 31 | 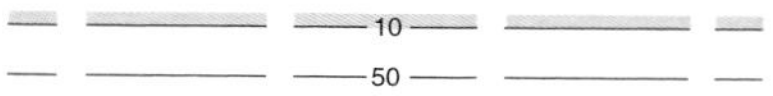 10<br>50 | *Approximate depth contours (length of dashes may vary)* | | 411.2<br>417.5 |

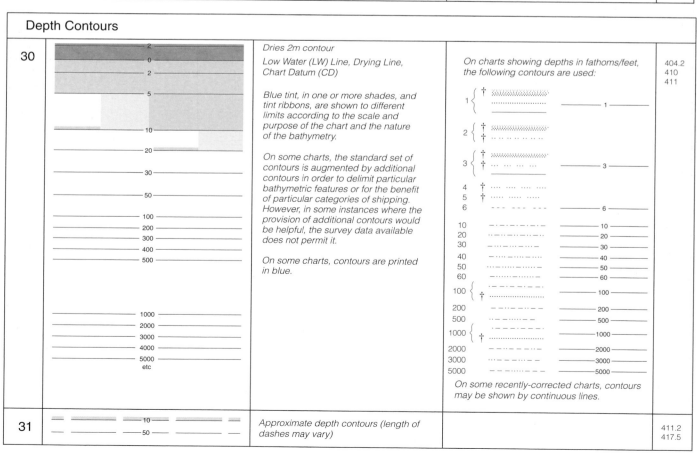

| | | | | | | |
|---|---|---|---|---|---|---|
| *Rocks* ⟶ K | | | | | Types of Seabed | |
| 1 | *S* | Sand | † | | s | 425-427 |
| 2 | *M* | Mud | † | | m | |
| 3 | *Cy* | Clay | † | | cl | |
| 4 | *Si* | Silt | | | | |
| 5 | *St* | Stones | † | | st | |
| 6 | *G* | Gravel | † | | g | |
| 7 | *P* | Pebbles | † | | peb | |
| 8 | *Cb* | Cobbles | | | | |
| 9.1 | *R* | Rock, Rocky | † | | r | |
| 9.2 | *Bo* | Boulder(s) | | | | 421.2 425-427 |
| 10 | *Co* | Coral | † | | crl | 425-427 |
| 11 | *Sh* | Shells | † | | sh | |
| 12.1 | *S/M* | Two layers e.g. Sand over Mud | #M (25)/SG   S (<1)/R *(Thickness of surface layer in metres)* | | | 425.8 |
| 12.2 | *fS.M.Sh* | *Mixed: where the seabed comprises a mixture of materials, the main constituent is given first, e.g. fine Sand with Mud and Shells* | | | | 425.9 |
| 13.1 | *Wd* | Weed (including Kelp) | † | | wd | 425.5 |
| 13.2 | ⪻⪻⪻ | Kelp | | | | 428.2 |
| 14 | ⌒ | Sandwaves | | | | 428.1 |
| 15 | ⁞ | Spring in seabed | | | | 428.3 |
| a | | Ground | † | *Gd* | grd | |
| b | | Ooze | † | *Oz* | | |
| c | | Marl | † | *Ml* | | |
| d | | Shingle | † | *Sn* | shin | |
| e | | Chalk | † | *Ck* | chk | |
| f | | Quartz | † | *Qz* | qrtz | |
| g | | Madrepore | † | *Md* | mad | |
| h | | Basalt | † | *Ba* | | |
| i | | Lava | † | *Lv* | | |
| j | | Pumice | † | *Pm* | pum | |
| k | | Tufa | † | *T* | | |
| l | | Scoriæ | † | *Sc* | | |
| m | | Cinders | † | *Cn* | cin | |

# J Nature of the Seabed

| n | | Manganese | † | Mn | man | |
|---|---|---|---|---|---|---|
| o | | Glauconite | † | Gc | | |
| p | | Oysters | † | Oy | oys | |
| q | | Mussels | † | Ms | mus | |
| r | | Sponge | † | Sp | | |
| s | | Algae | † | Al | | |
| t | | Foraminifera | † | Fr | for | |
| u | | Globigerina | † | Gl | | |
| v | | Diatoms | † | Di | | |
| w | | Radiolaria | † | Rd | rad | |
| x | | Pteropods | † | Pt | | |
| y | | Polyzoa | † | Po | pol | |

## Intertidal Areas

| 20 | | Area of sand and mud with patches of stones or gravel | | | 426.1 |
|---|---|---|---|---|---|
| 21 | | Rocky area | | | 426.2 |
| 22 | | Coral reef | | | 426.3 |

## Qualifying Terms

| 30 | f | Fine | | | | 425 427 |
|---|---|---|---|---|---|---|
| 31 | m | Medium — only used in relation to sand | | | | |
| 32 | c | Coarse | | | | |
| 33 | bk | Broken | † | brk | | |
| 34 | sy | Sticky | † | stk | | |
| 35 | so | Soft | † | sft | | |
| 36 | sf | Stiff | † | stf | | |
| 37 | v | Volcanic | † | vol | | |
| 38 | ca | Calcareous | † | cal | | |
| 39 | h | Hard | | | | 425.5 425.7 |

| aa | | Small | † | | sm | |
|----|---|-------|---|---|----|---|
| ab | | Large | † | | l | |
| ac | | Glacial | † | ga | glac | |
| ad | | Speckled | † | sk | spk | |
| ae | | White | † | | w | |
| af | | Black | † | bl | blk | |
| ag | | Blue | † | | b | |
| ah | | Green | † | | gn | |
| ai | | Yellow | † | | y | |
| aj | | Red | † | | rd | |
| ak | | Brown | † | | br | |
| al | | Chocolate | † | ch | choc | |
| am | | Grey | † | | gy | |
| an | | Light | † | | lt | |
| ao | | Dark | † | | d | |

# K Rocks, Wrecks, Obstructions

## General

| | | | | | |
|---|---|---|---|---|---|
| 1 | | Dangerline: A danger line draws attention to a danger which would not stand out clearly enough if represented solely by its symbol (e.g. isolated rock) or delimits an area containing numerous dangers, through which it is unsafe to navigate | | | 411.4 420.1 |
| 2 | $\underline{7_5}$ | Depth cleared by wire drag sweep or diver. The symbol may be used with other symbols, e.g. wrecks, obstructions, wells | | | 415 422.3 422.9 |
| 3 | $\overset{.....}{(12)}$ | Safe clearance depth. Obstruction over which the exact depth is unknown, but which is estimated to have a safe clearance at the depth shown. The symbol may be used with other symbols, e.g. wrecks, wells, turbines | | | 422.5 422.7 422.9 |
| a | | Dries | † Dr | † dr | |
| b | | Covers | † cov | | |
| c | | Uncovers | † uncov | | |

## Rocks

**Plane of Reference for Heights → H**     **Plane of Reference for Depths → H**

| | | | | |
|---|---|---|---|---|
| 10 | | Rock (islet) which does not cover, height above height datum | (1,7)     (3,1)     (4,1) <br> # | 421.1 |
| 11 | | Rock which covers and uncovers, height above Chart Datum, where known | † Dries 1·6m     † Dr 1·6m | 421.2 |
| 12 | | Rock awash at the level of Chart Datum | | 421.3 |
| 13 | | Underwater rock over which the depth is unknown, but which is considered dangerous to surface navigation | | 421.4 |
| 14 | | Underwater rock of known depth: | | 421.4 |
| 14.1 | | inside the corresponding depth area | | |
| 14.2 | | outside the corresponding depth area, dangerous to surface navigation | | |

28

| 15 | 35 / R | Underwater rock of known depth, not dangerous to surface navigation | | | 421.4 |
|----|---------|------------------------------------------------------------------------|---|---|-------|
| 16 | + Co + / + Co / + $5_8$ | Coral reef which is always covered | | | 421.5 |
| 17 | ⌣⌣ 18 $5_8$ 19 Br | Breakers | | | 423.2 |
| d | | Discoloured water | Discol | † Discold | 424.6 |

| | *Hulk → F* | *Plane of Reference for Depths → H* | *Historic Wreck → N*  **Wrecks and Fouls** | | |
|----|-----------|--------------------------------------|--------------------------------------|---|---|
| 20 | Mast (1·2) / Wk | Wreck, hull never covers, on large-scale charts | | | 422.1 |
| 21 | Mast ($1_2$) / Wk | Wreck, hull covers and uncovers, on large-scale charts | Wk † | Wk † | 422.1 |
| 22 | $5_2$ Wk    $6_5$ Wk | Submerged wreck, depth known, on large-scale charts | $5_2$ Wk † | | 422.1 |
| 23 | Wk | Submerged wreck, depth unknown, on large-scale charts | Wk † | | 422.1 |
| 24 | | Wreck showing any part of hull or superstructure at the level of Chart Datum | | | 422.2 |
| 25 | Masts | Wreck of which the mast(s) only are visible at Chart Datum | Mast (1·2) / Wk  Funnel / Mast ($1_2$) | | 422.2 |
| 26 | $4_6$ Wk    $25$ Wk | Wreck over which the depth has been obtained by sounding but not by wire sweep | | | 422.4 |
| 27 | $4_6$ Wk    $25$ Wk | Wreck, least depth obtained by wire sweep or diver | | | 422.3 |
| 28 | | Wreck, depth unknown, which is considered potentially dangerous to surface navigation | | | 422.6 |
| 29 | +++ | Wreck, in over 200m or depth unknown, which is considered not dangerous to surface navigation. For information about depth criteria, which may vary, see NP100, The Mariner's Handbook | | | 422.6 |
| e | | Submerged wreck, depth unknown | Wk † | | |

| | | | | |
|---|---|---|---|---|
| 30 | $\overline{20}$ Wk | Wreck over which the exact depth is unknown, but which is estimated to have a safe clearance at the depth shown | | 422.5 422.7 |
| 31 | #        # (22) | Foul ground, not dangerous to surface navigation, but to be avoided by vessels anchoring, trawling, etc (eg remains of wreck, cleared platform). Foul ground with depth | † ◯ Foul        † 22 Foul | 422.8 |
| g | # ── # ── (#) | Area of foul ground | † ▭ Foul        † ⌐ Foul ⌐ | |
| f | | Navigation light on stranded wreck | ⤙ | |

| Obstructions and Aquaculture | | Plane of Reference for Depths → H  Kelp, Seaweed → J  Underwater Installations → L | | |
|---|---|---|---|---|
| 40 | Obstn        Obstn | Obstruction or danger to navigation the exact nature of which is not specified or has not been determined, depth unknown | | 422.9 |
| 41 | $4_6$ Obstn        $16_8$ Obstn | Obstruction, depth obtained by sounding but not wire sweep | | 422.9 |
| 42 | $4_6$ Obstn        $16_8$ Obstn | Obstruction, least depth obtained by wire sweep or diver | | 422.9 |
| 43.1 | Obstn        ⊤ ⊤ ⊤        # | Stumps of posts or piles, wholly submerged | | 327.5 |
| 43.2 | #        ⊺ | Submerged pile, stake, snag or stump (with exact position) | | |
| 44.1 | ⊔⊔⊔⊔⊔⊔    ⊔⊔⊔⊔ | Fishing stakes | † ⊥ ⊥ ⊥ ⊥ ⊥        † ····· | 447.1 |
| 44.2 | ⌐ ⌐ | Fish trap, fish weir, tunny nets | †        ⌐ ┐ | 447.2 |
| 45 | ⌐ Fish traps ⌐        ⌐ Tunny nets ⌐ | Fish trap area, tunny nets area | ── ── ── ──  (U.S. waters only) | 447.3 |
| 46.1 | ⬟ ⊂⊃        ⊂⊃ | Fish haven | | 447.5 |
| 46.2 | ⬟ ⊂⊃ $2_4$        ⊂⊃ $(2_4)$ | Fish haven, with minimum depth | | |
| 47 | ⌐ ◌ ⌐        ◌    ⌐ ◌ ⌐ | Shellfish beds | ⌐ Shellfish Beds ⌐        † | 447.4 |
| 48.1 | ⌐ ⊠ ⌐        ⊠ | Marine farm (on large-scale charts) | † ⌐ Fish farm ⌐        † ⌐ Fish cages ⌐ | 447.6 |
| 48.2 | ⊠        □ | Marine farm (on small-scale charts) | | |

| | | | | | |
|---|---|---|---|---|---|
| *Combined symbols → K (General)* | | *Areas, Limits → N* | | | **General** |
| 1 | *EKOFISK OILFIELD* | Name of oilfield or gasfield | | | 445.3 |
| 2 | ⊡ Z-44 | Platform with designation/name | † ★ | † ⊡ | 445.3 |
| 3 | ⊡ | Limit of safety zone around offshore installation | | | 439.2 445.6 |
| 4 | | Limit of development area | | | 445.7 |
| 5.1 | 人　人　人 18 | Wind turbine, floating wind turbine and wind turbine with vertical clearance | | | 445.8 |
| 5.2 | ⌀　⌀ | Wind farm | | | 445.9 |
| | ⌀　⌀ | Wind farm (floating) | | | |
| 6 | ⌀　⌀ | Wave farm | | | 445.12 |

| | | | | | |
|---|---|---|---|---|---|
| *Mooring Buoys → Q* | | | | | **Platforms and Moorings** |
| 10 | ⊡ | Production platform, Platform, Oil derrick | † ★ | † ⊡ | 445.2 |
| 11 | ⊡ Fla | Flare stack (at sea) | | | 445.2 |
| 12 | ⊡ SPM | Fixed Single Point Mooring, including Single Anchor Leg Mooring (SALM), Articulated Loading Column (ALC) | | | 445.2 445.4 |
| 13 | | Observation / research platform (with name) | ⊡ Name | | |
| 14 | ⊡ Ru　　⊡ Z-44 (ru) | Disused platform, with superstructure removed | | | 445.2 |
| 15 | | Artificial Island | ⬦⬦⬦⬦ Name | | |
| 16 | ⌂ | Floating Single Point Mooring, including Catenary Anchor Leg Mooring (CALM), Single Buoy Mooring (SBM) | | | 445.4 |
| 17 | ⌂ | Moored storage tanker including FSU and FPSO | | | 445.5 |
| 18 | ------⚓ | Mooring ground tackle for fixing floating structures | | | 431.6 |

| | | | | | |
|---|---|---|---|---|---|
| *Plane of Reference for Depths → H* | | *Obstructions → K* | | | **Underwater Installations** |
| 20 | _15_ Well　　○ Well | Production well, with depth where known | † | ○ Prod Well | 445.1 |
| 21.1 | ○ Well | Suspended well (wellhead and pipes projecting from the seabed) over which the depth is unknown | | | 445.1 |
| 21.2 | _15_ Well | Suspended well over which the depth is known | | | 445.1 |
| 21.3 | | Suspended well with height of wellhead above the sea floor | # | ○ Well (5.7) | |

| 22 | # | Site of cleared platform | | 422.8 |
|---|---|---|---|---|
| 23 | ⊙ Pipe    Pipe (1₈) | Above-water wellhead (lit and unlit). The drying height or height above height datum is charted if known | | 445.1 |
| 24 | Turbine    FL(2) ★ Underwater Turbine | Underwater turbine | | 445.10 445.11 |
| 25 | ODAS | Subsurface Ocean (or oceanographic) Data Aquisition System (ODAS) | | 448.4 |
| c | | Single Well Oil Production System. The depth shown is the least depth over the wellhead. For substantial periods of time a loading tanker is positioned over the wellhead | 93 SWOPS | 445.1 |
| d | | Underwater installations; template, manifold | Template    Manifold | 445.1 |

## Submarine Cables

| 30.1 | ~~~~~~~~~~~ | Submarine cable | † ~~~~~~~~~~~ | 443.1 443.8 |
|---|---|---|---|---|
| 30.2 | ⊤⊤⊤⊤ ~~~~ ⊤⊤⊤⊤ ⊥⊥⊥⊥ ~~~~ ⊥⊥⊥⊥ | Submarine cable area | † — — — Cable Area — — — | 439.3 443.2 |
| 31.1 | ~~~~~ ∫ ~~~~~ | Submarine power cable | † ~~~~ Power ~~~~ † ~~~~ Power ~~~~ | 443.2 |
| 31.2 | ⊤⊤⊤⊤ ~~∫~~ ⊤⊤⊤⊤ ⊥⊥⊥⊥ ~~∫~~ ⊥⊥⊥⊥ | Submarine power cable area | † — — Power Cable Area — — | 439.3 443.2 |
| 32 | ᴧᴧ ᴧ ᴧᴧ ~~~ ᴧᴧ ᴧᴧ | Disused submarine cable | | 443.7 |

## Submarine Pipelines

| 40.1 | →→→→→→→→→→→ Oil    Gas →→→→→→→ →→→→→→→ Chem    Water →→→→→→→ →→→→→→→ | Supply pipeline: unspecified, oil, gas, chemicals, water | † — — — Pipeline — — — | 444 444.1 |
|---|---|---|---|---|
| 40.2 | →→→⊤⊤⊤⊤⊤⊤⊤→→→ ←←←⊥⊥⊥⊥⊥⊥⊥←←← →→→⊤⊤⊤ ⊤⊤⊤→→→ Oil    Gas ←←←⊥⊥⊥ ⊥⊥⊥←←← →→→⊤⊤⊤ ⊤⊤⊤→→→ Chem    Water ←←←⊥⊥⊥ ⊥⊥⊥←←← | Supply pipeline area: unspecified, oil, gas, chemicals, water | † ⌐ Pipeline ¬    † ⌐ Pipeline ¬ ⌊ Area ⌋    ⌊ Area ⌋ | 439.3 444.3 |
| 41.1 | →→→→→→→→→→→→ Water    Sewer Outfall    Intake →→→→→→→→→→→→ | Outfall and intake: unspecified, water, sewer, outfall, intake | † - - - Sewer - - - † - - - Outfall - - - | 444 444.2 |
| 41.2 | →→⊤⊤⊤⊤⊤⊤⊤⊤→→ ←←⊥⊥⊥⊥⊥⊥⊥⊥←← →→⊤⊤⊤ ⊤⊤⊤→→ Water    Sewer ←←⊥⊥⊥ ⊥⊥⊥←← →→⊤⊤⊤ ⊤⊤⊤→→ Outfall    Intake ←←⊥⊥⊥ ⊥⊥⊥←← | Outfall and intake area: unspecified, water, sewer, outfall, intake | † ⌐ Pipeline ¬    † ⌐ Pipeline ¬ ⌊ Area ⌋    ⌊ Area ⌋ | 439.3 444.3 |
| 42.1 | →→→→ Buried 1·6m →→→→→→ | Buried pipeline / pipe (with nominal depth to which buried) | | 444.5 |
| 42.2 | →→→) (→→→ | Pipeline tunnel | | |
| 43 | →→→→→→→→→ 3₂ Obstn | Diffuser, crib | →→→→→→→→→ 3₂ Diffuser | 444.8 |
| 44 | →→ →→ →→ →→ → → → → → | Disused pipeline / pipe | | 444.7 |

| | | | | |
|---|---|---|---|---|
| *Tracks Marked by Lights* → P | | *Leading Beacons* → Q | | Tracks |
| 1 | 270·5° / 2 Bns ‡ 270·5° | Leading line ( ‡ means "in line", the continuous line is the track to be followed) | † Bn   Bn   *Bns in Line 270°30'* / Ldg Bns 270·5° / 270·5° | 433.1 433.2 433.3 |
| 2 | 270·5° / Island open of Headland 270·5° | Transit (other than leading line), Clearing line | Bns in line 270·5° | 433.4 433.5 |
| 3 | 090°-270° | Recommended track based on a system of fixed marks | † → / † ← → / ‡ | 434.1 434.2 |
| 4 | 090°-270° | Recommended track not based on a system of fixed marks ‡ | — < — DW — 270° — < — — | 434.1 434.2 |
| 5.1 | DW (see Note) | One-way track and DW track based on a system of fixed marks | † ← / † ← | 432.3 434.1 |
| 5.2 | 270° DW | One-way track and DW track not based on a system of fixed marks | | |
| 6 | < 7·3m > / < 7·3m > ‡ | Recommended track with maximum authorised draught | | 432.4 434.3 434.4 |

| | | | | |
|---|---|---|---|---|
| | | **Routeing Measures - Basic Symbols** | | |
| 10 | ⇒ | Established (mandatory) direction of traffic flow | | 435.1 |
| 11 | ⇒ ‡ | Recommended direction of traffic flow | | 435.5 |
| 12 | | Separation line (large-scale, small-scale) | | 435.1 436.3 |
| 13 | | Separation zone | | 435.1 436.3 |
| 14 | | Limit of restricted routeing measure (e.g. Inshore Traffic Zone, Area to be Avoided) | | 435.1 436.3 439.2 |
| 15 | | Limit of routeing measure | | 435.1 436.3 |
| 16 | ⚠ / Precautionary Area | Precautionary area | | 435.2 |
| 17 | ASL (see Note) | Archipelagic Sea Lane; axis line and limit beyond which vessels shall not navigate | ASL (see Note) † | 435.10 |
| 18 | FAIRWAY 7.3m / FAIRWAY <7.3m> | Fairway, designated by regulatory authority: with minimum depth / with maximum authorised draught | | 434.5 |

‡ *The term 'recommended' in connection with tracks and routeing measures does not imply recommendation by the United Kingdom Hydrographic Office. It is usually by a regulatory authority, but may be established by precedent.*

# M Tracks, Routes

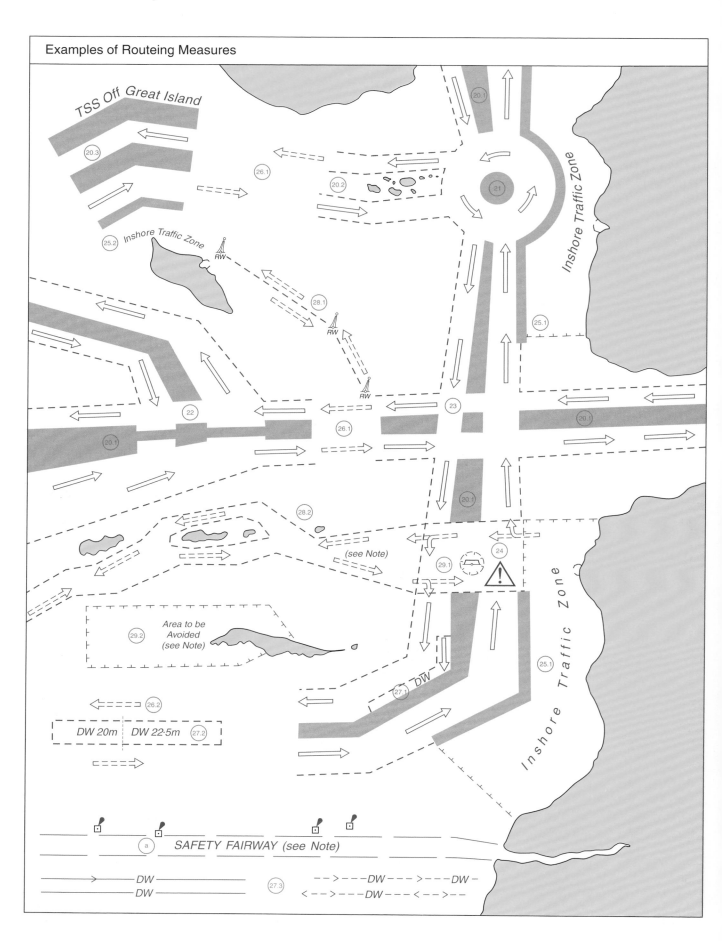

Examples of Routeing Measures

## Examples of Routeing Measures (see diagram on page 34)

| | | |
|---|---|---|
| (20.1) | Traffic separation scheme (TSS), traffic separated by separation zone | 435.1 |
| (20.2) | Traffic separation scheme, traffic separated by natural obstructions | 435.1 |
| (20.3) | Traffic separation scheme, with outer separation zone, separating traffic using scheme from traffic not using it | 435.1 |
| (21) | Traffic separation scheme, roundabout | 435.1 |
| (22) | Traffic separation scheme with "crossing gates" | 435.1 |
| (23) | Traffic separation schemes crossing, without designated precautionary area | 435.1 |
| (24) | Precautionary area | 435.2 |
| (25.1) | Inshore traffic zone (ITZ), with defined end limits | 435.1 |
| (25.2) | Inshore traffic zone, without defined end limits | 435.1 |
| ‡ (26.1) | Recommended direction of traffic flow, between traffic separation schemes | 435.5 |
| ‡ (26.2) | Recommended direction of traffic flow, for ships not needing a deep water route | 435.5 |
| (27.1) | Deep water route (DW), as part of one-way traffic lane | 435.3 |
| (27.2) | Two-way deep water route, with minimum depth stated | 435.3 |
| (27.3) | Deep water route, centre line shown as recommended one-way or two-way track | 435.3 |
| ‡ (28.1) | Recommended route (often marked by centre line buoys) | 435.4 |
| (28.2) | Two-way route with one-way sections | 435.6 |
| (29.1) | Area to be avoided (ATBA), around navigational aid | 435.7 |
| (29.2) | Area to be avoided, because of danger of stranding | 435.7 |
| (a) | Safety fairway | 432.2 |

‡ The term 'recommended' in connection with tracks and routeing measures does not imply recommendation by the United Kingdom Hydrographic Office. It is usually by a regulatory authority, but may be established by precedent.

## Radar Surveillance System

| | | | | |
|---|---|---|---|---|
| 30 | ⊙ Radar Surveillance Station | Radar surveillance station | | 487 487.3 |
| 31 | Ra Cuxhaven | Radar range | | 487.1 |
| 32.1 | ————— Ra ————— | Radar reference line | | 487.2 |
| 32.2 | Ra    090° - 270° | Radar reference line coinciding with a leading line | | |

## Radio Reporting

| | | | | | |
|---|---|---|---|---|---|
| 40.1 | B / 7 | Radio calling-in point, way point, or reporting point (with designation, if any) showing direction(s) of vessel movement | ‡ | B / 7 | 488.1 |
| 40.2 | – –◊– – – – – – –◊– – | Radio reporting line (with designation, if any) showing direction(s) of vessel movement | ‡ | ‡ | 488.2 |

## Ferries

| | | | | |
|---|---|---|---|---|
| 50 | ———–○——— | Ferry Route | ‡ Ferry / ‡ Ferry | 438.1 |
| 51 | Cable Ferry ———○——— | Cable Ferry Route | | 438.2 |

# N Areas, Limits

| General | Dredged and Swept Areas → I | Submarine Cables, Submarine Pipelines → L | Tracks Routes → M |
|---|---|---|---|

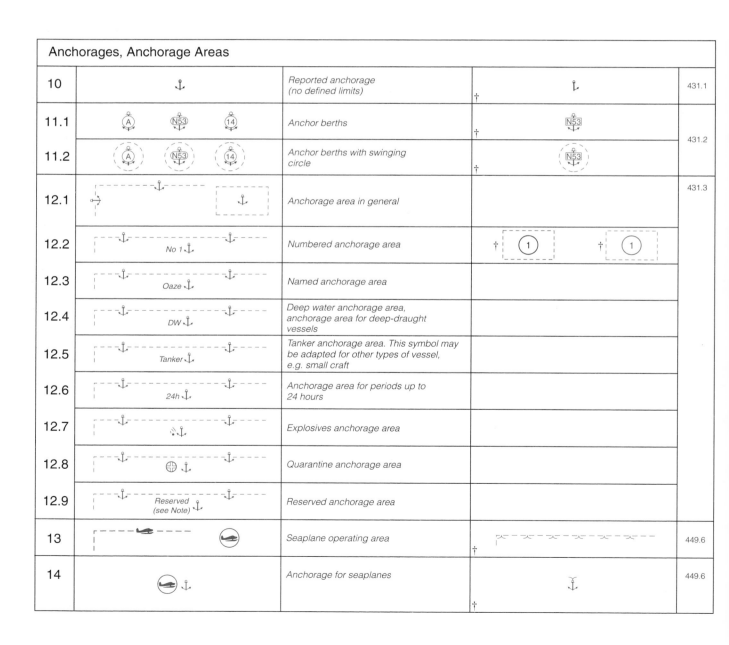

| | | | | |
|---|---|---|---|---|
| 1.1 | | Maritime limit in general, usually implying permanent physical obstructions *(for emphasis)* | | 439.1 439.6 |
| 1.2 | | Maritime limit in general, usually implying no permanent physical obstructions *(for emphasis)* | | |
| 2.1 | | Limit of restricted area *(for emphasis)* | | 439.2 439.3 439.6 441.6 |
| 2.2 | | Limit of area into which entry is prohibited | † Entry Prohibited | |

## Anchorages, Anchorage Areas

| | | | | |
|---|---|---|---|---|
| 10 | | Reported anchorage (no defined limits) | † | 431.1 |
| 11.1 | Ⓐ N53 14 | Anchor berths | † N53 | 431.2 |
| 11.2 | Ⓐ N53 14 | Anchor berths with swinging circle | † N53 | |
| 12.1 | | Anchorage area in general | | 431.3 |
| 12.2 | No 1 | Numbered anchorage area | † ① † ① | |
| 12.3 | Oaze | Named anchorage area | | |
| 12.4 | DW | Deep water anchorage area, anchorage area for deep-draught vessels | | |
| 12.5 | Tanker | Tanker anchorage area. This symbol may be adapted for other types of vessel, e.g. small craft | | |
| 12.6 | 24h | Anchorage area for periods up to 24 hours | | |
| 12.7 | | Explosives anchorage area | | |
| 12.8 | ⊕ | Quarantine anchorage area | | |
| 12.9 | Reserved (see Note) | Reserved anchorage area | | |
| 13 | | Seaplane operating area | † | 449.6 |
| 14 | | Anchorage for seaplanes | † | 449.6 |

| | | | | |
|---|---|---|---|---|
| | | | Restricted Areas | |
| 20 | | Anchoring prohibited | Anchoring Prohibited † ‖ † | 431.4 435.11 439.3 439.4 |
| 21 | | Fishing prohibited | | 439.3 439.4 |
| 22 | Examples ⊤ ⊤ MR ⊤ ⊤ ⊤ MR ⊤ ⊤ ⊤ ⊤ ⊤ MR ⊤ ⊤ ⊤ MR ⊤ ⊤ | Environmentally Sensitive Sea Areas: (colour may be green or magenta) Limit of marine reserve, national park, non-specific nature reserve | Marine Nature Reserve (see Note) † | 437.3 437.6 437.7 |
| | Examples | Bird sanctuary, seal sanctuary (other animal silhouettes may be used for specialized areas) | # | |
| | PSSA PSSA | Particularly Sensitive Sea Area (coloured tint band may vary in width between 1 and 5mm) | | |
| 23.1 | Explosives Dumping Ground | Explosives dumping ground, individual mine or explosive | Explosives Dumping Ground † | 442.1 442.2 442.3 442.4 |
| 23.2 | Explosives Dumping Ground (disused) | Explosives dumping ground (disused) | Explosives Dumping Ground (disused) † | |
| 24 | Dumping Ground for Chemicals | Dumping ground for chemical waste | | 442.1 442.2 442.3 |
| 25 | Degaussing Range | Degaussing range | † D.G. Range DG Range | 448.1 448.2 |
| 27 | 5kn | Maximum speed, speed limit | | 430.2 |
| a | | Seabed operations dangerous/prohibited | # | |
| b | | Diving dangerous/prohibited | # | |
| | | | Military Practice Areas | |
| 30 | | Firing practice area | | 441.1 441.2 441.3 |
| 31 | | Military restricted area into which entry is prohibited | Entry Prohibited † | 441.6 |
| 32 | | Mine-laying (and counter-measure) practice area | | 441.4 |
| 33 | SUBMARINE EXERCISE AREA | Submarine transit lane and exercise area | | 441.5 |
| 34 | Minefield | Minefield | Mine Danger Area (see Note) | 441.8 |

# N    Areas, Limits

## International Boundaries and National Limits

| | | | | |
|---|---|---|---|---|
| 40 | DANMARK ++++++++++++++++++++++++ DEUTSCHLAND | International boundary on land | † DENMARK ++++++++++++++++++++++ GERMANY | 440.1 |
| 41 | UNITED KINGDOM — + — + — + — + — + — + — + NORGE | International maritime boundary | † UNITED KINGDOM — + — + — + — + — + — + NORWAY   † Continental Shelf — — — — — — — — — Boundary | 440.3 |
| 42 | Straight territorial sea baseline diagram | Straight territorial sea baseline with base point | | 440.4 |
| 43 | ——————— + + ——————— | Seaward limit of Territorial Sea | # +++++++++++++++++++++++ | 440.5 |
| 44 | ——————— + ——————— | Seaward limit of Contiguous Zone | | 440.6 |
| 45 | — ⋈ — — — ⋈ —   — ⋈ — — — — ⋈ — | National fishery limits | | 440.7 |
| 46 | ——— Continental Shelf ——— | Limit of Continental Shelf | | 440.8 |
| 47 | ——— EEZ ——— | Limit of Exclusive Economic Zone | # ——— + + ——————— + + ——— | 440.9 |
| 48 | — — ⊖ — — — — — ⊖ — — | Customs limit | | 440.2 |
| 49 | Harbour Limit | Harbour limit | † Harbour Limit | 430.1 |

## Various Limits

| | | | | |
|---|---|---|---|---|
| 60.1 | (2008) # | ⋎⋎⋎⋎⋎ | Limit of fast ice, Ice front (with date) | 449.1 |
| 60.2 | (2008) # | ⋎⋎⋎⋎⋎ | Limit of sea ice (pack ice) seasonal (with date) | † |
| 61 | Log Pond | | Floating barrier, including log ponds, security barriers, ice booms, shark nets | † Booming Ground     † Timber | 449.2 |
| 62.1 | Spoil Ground | | Spoil ground | | 446.1 446.2 |
| 62.2 | Spoil Ground (disused) | | Spoil ground (disused) | | |
| 63 | Extraction Area | | Extraction (dredging) area | † Dredging Area | 446.4 |
| 64 | Cargo Transhipment Area | | Cargo transhipment area | | 449.4 |
| 65 | † Incineration Area | | Incineration area | † Area for burning refuse material | 449.3 |

| | | | | | |
|---|---|---|---|---|---|
| Beacons → Q | | | Light Structures, Major Floating Lights | | |
| 1 | ⭐ ⭐   Lt      LtHo | Major light, minor light ‡, light, lighthouse | # | | 470.5 |
| 2 | | Lighted offshore platform | | | 445.2 |
| 3 | BY     ⭐ BnTr | Lighted beacon tower ‡ | † Bn Tower     † Bn Tr | | 456.4 457.1 457.2 |
| 4 | R    BRB    ⭐ Bn | Lighted beacon ‡ On smaller scale charts, where navigation within recognition range of the daymark is unlikely, lighted beacons are charted solely as lights | R    BRB    G    R    # | | 457.1 457.2 |
| 5 | R    ⭐ Bn | Lighted buoyant beacon, resilient beacon ‡ | | | 459.1 459.2 |
| 6 | | Major floating light (light vessel, major light float, Large Automatic Navigational Buoy (LANBY)) | †    LtV | | 462.9 474 |
| 7 | | Navigation lights on landmarks or other structures | | | 470.5 |

‡ Minor lights, fixed and floating, usually conform to IALA Maritime Buoyage System characteristics

| | | |
|---|---|---|
| | Bearings of Light Off Chart Limits | |
| 8 | 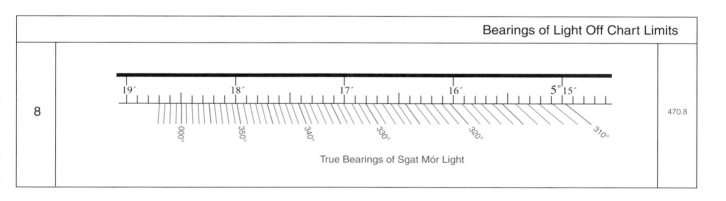 True Bearings of Sgat Mór Light | 470.8 |

# P  Lights

| Light Characters | | | | Light Characters on Light Buoys → Q | 471.2 |

| | Abbreviation | | Class of Light | Illustration | Period shown ⊢—— |
|---|---|---|---|---|---|
| | International | National | | | |
| **10.1** | F | | *Fixed* | | |
| **10.2** | *Occulting (total duration of light longer than total duration of darkness)* | | | | |
| | Oc | Occ † | *Single-occulting* | | |
| | Oc(2) *Example* | GpOcc(2) *Example* † | *Group-occulting* | | |
| | Oc(2+3) *Example* | GpOcc(2+3) *Example* † | *Composite group-occulting* | | |
| **10.3** | *Isophase (duration of light and darkness equal)* | | | | |
| | Iso | | *Isophase* | | |
| **10.4** | *Flashing (total duration of light shorter than total duration of darkness)* | | | | |
| | Fl | | *Single-flashing* | | |
| | Fl(3) *Example* | GpFl(3) *Example* † | *Group-flashing* | | |
| | Fl(2+1) *Example* | GpFl(2+1) *Example* † | *Composite group-flashing* | | |
| **10.5** | LFl | | *Long-flashing (flash 2s or longer)* | | |
| **10.6** | *Quick (repetition rate of 50 to 79 - usually either 50 or 60 - flashes per minute)* | | | | |
| | Q | QkFl † | *Continuous quick* | | |
| | Q(3) *Example* | QkFl(3) *Example* † | *Group quick* | | |
| | IQ | IntQkFl † | *Interrupted quick* | | |
| **10.7** | *Very quick (repetition rate of 80 to 159 - usually either 100 or 120 - flashes per minute)* | | | | |
| | VQ | VQkFl † | *Continuous very quick* | | |
| | VQ(3) *Example* | VQkFl(3) *Example* † | *Group very quick* | | |
| | IVQ | IntVQkFl † | *Interrupted very quick* | | |
| **10.8** | *Ultra quick (repetition rate of 160 or more - usually 240 to 300 - flashes per minute)* | | | | |
| | UQ | | *Continuous ultra quick* | | |
| | IUQ | | *Interrupted ultra quick* | | |
| **10.9** | Mo(K) *Example* | | *Morse Code* | | |
| **10.10** | FFl | | *Fixed and flashing* | | |
| **10.11** | Al.WR *Example* | Alt.WR *Example* † | *Alternating* | | |

## Colours of Lights and Marks

| | | | | | |
|---|---|---|---|---|---|
| 11.1 | W | | White (for lights, only on sector and alternating lights) | | 450.2 450.3 470.4 |
| 11.2 | R | | Red | | 470.6 471.4 |
| 11.3 | G | | Green | | 475.1 |
| 11.4 | Bu | | Blue | † | Bl |
| 11.5 | Vi | | Violet | | |
| 11.6 | Y | | Yellow | | |
| 11.7 | Y # | Or | Orange | † | Or |
| 11.8 | Y # | Am | Amber | | |

Colours of lights shown on:

standard charts

on multicoloured charts

on multicoloured charts at sector lights

## Period

| | | | | | |
|---|---|---|---|---|---|
| 12 | 90s *Examples* | 2·5s | Period in seconds and tenths of a second | † | 90sec | 471.5 |

*Plane of Reference for Heights → H*    *Tidal Levels → H*

## Elevation

| | | | | |
|---|---|---|---|---|
| 13 | 12m *Example* | Elevation of light given in metres | On fathoms charts, the elevation of a light is given in feet e.g. **40ft** | 471.6 |

*Note: Charted ranges are nominal ranges given in sea miles*

## Range

| | | | | |
|---|---|---|---|---|
| 14 | 15M *Example* | Light with single range | | 471.7 471.9 475.5 |
| | 15/10M *Example* | Light with two different ranges | † 15,10M | |
| | 15-7M *Example* | Light with three or more ranges | † 15,10,7M | |

## Disposition

| | | | | |
|---|---|---|---|---|
| 15 | (hor) | horizontally disposed | † (horl.) | |
| | (vert) | vertically disposed | † (vertl.) | 471.8 |
| | (△)        (▽) | 3 lights disposed in the shape of a triangle | | |

## Example of a full Light Description    471.9

| 16 | |
|---|---|

**Example** *of a light description on a* **metric** *chart using international abbreviations:* ★ Fl(3)WRG.15s13m7-5M

| | |
|---|---|
| Fl(3) | **Class** or **character** of light: in this example a group-flashing light, regularly repeating a group of three flashes. |
| WRG. | **Colours** of light: white, red and green, exhibiting the different colours in defined sectors. |
| 15s | **Period** of light in seconds, i.e., the time taken to exhibit one full sequence of 3 flashes and eclipses: 15 seconds. |
| 13m | **Elevation** of focal plane above height datum: 13 metres. |
| 7-5M | **Luminous range** in sea miles: the distance at which a light of a particular intensity can be seen in 'clear' visibilty, taking no account of earth curvature. In those countries (eg United Kingdom) where the term 'clear' is defined as a meteorological visibilty of 10 sea miles, the range may be termed "**nominal**". In this example the ranges of the colours are: white 7 miles, green 5 miles, red between 7 and 5 miles. |

**Example** *of a light description on a* **fathoms** *chart using international abbreviations:* ★ Al.Fl.WR.30s110ft23/22M

| | |
|---|---|
| Al.Fl. | **Class** or **character** of light: in this example exhibiting single flashes of differing colours alternately. |
| WR. | **Colours** of light shown alternately: white and red all-round (ie, not a sector light). |
| 30s | **Period** of light in seconds, ie, the time taken to exhibit the sequence of two flashes and two eclipses: 30 seconds. |
| 110ft | **Elevation** of focal plane above height datum: 110 feet. |
| 23/22M | **Range** in sea miles. Until 1971 the lesser of **geographical** range (based on a height of eye of 15 feet) and **luminous** range was charted. Now, when the charts are corrected, luminous (or nominal) range is given. In this example the luminous ranges of the colours are: white 23 miles, red 22 miles. The geographical range can be found from the table in the Admiralty List of Lights (for the elevation of 110 feet, it would be 16 miles). |

# P Lights

| Lights marking Fairways | Note: Quoted bearings are always from seaward |
|---|---|

## Leading Lights and Lights in line

| | | | | |
|---|---|---|---|---|
| 20.1 | Oc.6s / Oc.3s 225.3° / Oc.3s8m12M / Oc.6s24m15M | Leading lights with leading line (the firm line is the track to be followed) and arcs of visibility | Oc.6s / Oc.3s / Ldg Lts 225.3° / Oc.3s8m12M / Oc.6s24m15M † | 433 433.1 433.2 433.3 475.1 475.6 |
| 20.2 | Oc.4s12M / Oc.R. 4s10M / Oc&Oc.R ≠ 269·3° | Leading lights ( ≠ means "in line"; the firm line is the track to be followed; the light descriptions will be at the light stars or on the leading line, not usually both). | Occ.4s12M / Occ.R. 4s10M / Lights in line 269°18′ † | 433.2 433.3 475.6 |
| 20.3 | LdgOc.W&R | Leading lights on small-scale charts | Oc.W&R 265° | 433.1 475.6 |
| 21 | Fl.G / Fl.G / 2Fl.R 270° / 270° | Lights in line (marking the sides of a channel) | Lights in line 092° / Fl Fl † | 433.4 475.6 |
| 22 | Rear Lt or Upper Lt | Rear or upper light | Upr. † | 470.7 |
| 23 | Front Lt or Lower Lt | Front or lower light | Lr † | 470.7 |

## Direction Lights

| | | | | |
|---|---|---|---|---|
| 30.1 | Dir 269° / Fl(2)5s10m11M | Direction light with narrow sector and course to be followed, flanked by darkness or unintensified light | DirLt † | |
| 30.2 | Oc.12s6M / Dir 299° / Dir 255·5° / Fl(2)15s11M | Direction light with course to be followed. Sector(s) uncharted | DirLt † | 471.3 471.9 475 475.1 475.5 475.7 |
| 30.3 | F.G / Al.WG / Oc.W.4s / Al.WR / F.R / DirWRG. 15-5M | Direction light with narrow fairway sector flanked by light sectors of different characters on standard charts | | |
| 30.4 | F.G / Al.WG / Oc.W.4s / Al.WR / F.R / DirWRG. 15-5M # | Direction light with narrow fairway sector flanked by light sectors of different characters on multicoloured charts | | |
| 31 | Dir 286° | Moiré effect light (day and night), variable arrow mark. Arrows show when course alteration needed | | 475.8 |

| | | Sector Lights | | |
|---|---|---|---|---|
| 40.1 | Fl.WRG.4s21m 18-12M | *Sector light on standard charts* | | 475 475.1 475.2 475.5 |
| 40.2 | Fl.WRG.4s21m 18-12M | *Sector light on multicoloured charts* | | |
| 41.1 | Oc.WRG. 10-6M | *Sector lights on standard charts, the white sector limits marking the sides of the fairway* | | 475 475.1 475.5 470.4 |
| 41.2 | Oc.WRG. 10-6M | *Sector lights on multicoloured charts, the white sector limits marking the sides of the fairway* | | |
| 42 | Fl(3)10s62m25M F.R.55m12M | *Main light visible all-round with red subsidiary light seen over danger* | | 471.8 475.4 |
| 43 | Fl.5s41m30M | *All-round light with obscured sector* | Fl.5s41m30M | 475.3 |
| 44 | Iso.WRG | *Light with arc of visibility deliberately restricted* | | 475.3 |
| 45 | Q.14m5M | *Light with faint sector* | | 475.3 |
| 46 | Oc.R.8s  Oc.R.8s5M | *Light with intensified sector* | | 475.2 |
| c | | *Light with unintensified sector* | Oc.R.8s  Oc.R.8s5/2M | |

# P Lights

## Lights with limited Times of Exhibition

| 50 | ☆ F.R(occas) | Lights exhibited only when specially needed (e.g. for fishing vessels, ferries) and some private lights | † (fishg.)  † (Priv.)  † (occasl.) | 473.2 |
|---|---|---|---|---|
| 51 | ☆ Fl.10s40m27M (F.37m11M Day) | Daytime light (charted only where the character shown by day differs from that shown at night) | † ☆ Fl.10s40m27M (F.37m11M by Day) | 473.4 |
| 52 | ☆ Q.WRG.5m10-3M (Fl.5s Fog) | Fog light (exhibited only in fog, or character changes in fog) | † ☆ Q.WRG.5m10-3M Fl.5s (in Fog) | 473.5 |
| 53 | ☆ Fl.5s(U)  † | Unwatched (unmanned) light with no standby or emergency arrangements | | 473.1 |
| 54 | (temp)  # | Temporary | † (temp)          † (tempy.) | 473.6 |
| 55 | (exting) | Extinguished | † (extingd.) | 473.7 |

## Special Lights        Flare Stack (at Sea) → L        Flare Stack (on Land) → E        Signal Stations → T

| 60 | ☆ AeroAl.Fl.WG.7·5s11M | Aero light (may be unreliable) | | 476.1 |
|---|---|---|---|---|
| 61.1 | ☆ AeroF.R.353m11M RADIO MAST (353)  † | Air obstruction light of high intensity | | 476.2 |
| 61.2 | (89) (R Lts) | Air obstruction lights (eg on radio mast) | † (Red Lt.) | |
| 62 | Fog Det Lt | Fog detector light | | 477 |
| 63 | ◁▷        ◁▷ (illuminated) | Floodlit, floodlighting of a structure | (illum)          † (lit) | 478.2 |
| 64 | F        Iso  F.R | Strip light | | 478.5 |
| 65 | (priv)  # | Private light other than one exhibited occasionally | #  ⊙ Y.Lt   #  ⊙ R.Lt        † (Priv) | 473.2 |
| 66 | (sync) or (sync) | Synchronized (synchronous or sequential) | | 478.3 |

| | | | | |
|---|---|---|---|---|
| IALA Maritime Buoyage System, which includes Beacons → Q 130 | | | Buoys and Beacons | |

### General

| 1 | —○— | Position of buoy or beacon | | 455.3 460.1 462.1 |
|---|---|---|---|---|

### Colour of Buoys and Beacons

Abbreviations for colours (lights) → P 11

| 2 | G  B  G  G  G | Single colour; green (G) and black (B) | † | B           G | 450 450.1 450.2 450.3 464 464.1 464.2 464.3 |
|---|---|---|---|---|---|
| 3 | R  R  Y  Y  Or  R | Single colour other than green and black: red (R), yellow (Y), orange (Or) | † | R      Y      Or | |
| 4 | BY  GRG  BRB | Multiple colours in horizontal bands: the colour sequence is from top to bottom | † | BW   RW   BR   BW | |
| 5 | RW  RW  BuY  RW | Multiple colours in vertical or diagonal stripes; the darker colour is given first. In these examples, red (R), white(W), blue (Bu), yellow (Y) & black(B) | † | RW   BR   BW   BW | |
| 6 | | Retroreflecting material may be fitted to some unlit marks. Charts do not usually show it. Black bands will appear dark blue under a spotlight | † | Refl | |
| a | | Single colour other than green and black (non-IALA system: white (W) grey (Gy), blue (Bu)) | † | W     Gy     Bu <br> W (non-IALA)   Gy (non-IALA)   Bu (non-IALA) | 464 |
| b | | Wreck buoy (not used in the IALA System) | † | G      G      G      G | |
| c | | Chequered | † | BR   BW   RW   BW | |

### Lighted Marks

Marks with Fog Signals → R

| 7 | Fl.G  G      Fl.R  R | Lighted marks on standard charts (examples) | † |           | 457.1 466 466.1 |
|---|---|---|---|---|---|
| 8 | Fl.R  R      Iso  RW      Fl.G  G | Lighted marks on multicoloured charts (examples) | | | |

### Topmarks and Radar Reflectors

For Application of Topmarks within the IALA System → Q 130     Radar reflector → S

| 9 | (topmark symbols) | IALA System buoy topmarks (beacon topmarks shown upright) | Non-IALA System # (topmark symbols) etc. | | | 463 463.1 |
|---|---|---|---|---|---|---|
| 10 | Name R  2 | Beacon with topmark, colour, radar reflector and designation (example) | '2' R | No.2 R | Ra.Refl "2" † | 450 455.2 455.7 |
| 11 | Name G  3 | Buoy with topmark, colour, radar reflector and designation (example). Radar reflectors are not generally charted on IALA System buoys | '3' G | No.3 | Ra.Refl "No.3" † | 460.3 460.6 465.1 465.2 |

# Q  Buoys, Beacons

| Buoys | *Features Common to Beacons and Buoys* $\longrightarrow$ Q 1-11 |

## Shapes

| 20 | | | Conical buoy, nun buoy, ogival buoy | † | | | *etc.* | 462.2 |
|---|---|---|---|---|---|---|---|---|
| 21 | | | Can buoy, cylindrical buoy | † | | | *etc.* | 462.3 |
| 22 | | | Spherical buoy | † | | | *etc.* | 462.4 |
| 23 | | | | Pillar buoy | † | | | 462.5 |
| 24 | | | Spar buoy, spindle buoy | † | | | | | 462.6 |
| 25 | | | Barrel buoy, tun buoy | | | 462.7 |
| 26 | | | Superbuoy. Superbuoys are very large buoys, e.g. a LANBY (P6) is a navigational aid mounted on a circular hull of about 5m diameter. Oil or gas installation buoys (L16) and ODAS buoys (Q58), of similar size, are shown by variations of the superbuoy symbol | † | | 445.4<br>460.4<br>462.9<br>474 |

## Minor Light Floats

| 30 | Fl.G.3s / G Name | Light float as part of IALA System | | 462.8 |
|---|---|---|---|---|
| 31 | † Fl.10s | Light float not part of IALA System | † B R B | 462.8 |

## Mooring Buoys

| Mooring Buoys | *Oil or Gas Installation Buoy* $\longrightarrow$ L | *Visitors' (Small Craft) Mooring* $\longrightarrow$ U |

| 40 | # # # | Mooring buoy | # # # † | 431.5 |
|---|---|---|---|---|
| 41 | Fl.Y.2·5s | Lighted mooring buoy (example) | | 431.5<br>466.1<br>466.2<br>466.3<br>466.4 |
| 42 | ①  ② | Trot, mooring buoys with ground tackle and berth numbers | ①  ② † | 323.1<br>431.6 |
| 43 | ~~~~~~~ | Mooring buoy with telegraphic or telephonic communications | | 431.5 |
| 44 | Small Craft Moorings | Numerous moorings (example) | | 431.7 |
| 45 | V | Visitor's mooring | | 431.5 |

*The symbols shown below are examples: shapes of buoys may differ; lateral or cardinal buoys may be used in some situations; the use of the cross topmark is optional.*

### Special Purpose Buoys

| No. | Symbol | Description | | Ref. |
|---|---|---|---|---|
| 50 | ⚲ DZ | Firing danger area (Danger Zone) buoy | | 441.2 |
| 51 | ⚲ Target | Target | | |
| 52 | ⚲ Marker Ship | Marker Ship | | |
| 53 | ⚲ Barge | Barge | | |
| 54 | ⚲ DG | Degaussing Range buoy | | 448.2 |
| 55 | ⚲ Cable | Cable buoy | ⚲ Cable † | 443.6 |
| 56 | ⚲ | Spoil ground buoy | | 446.3 |
| 57 | ⚲ | Buoy marking outfall | | 444.4 |
| 58 | ⌑ ODAS    ⚲ ODAS | Ocean (or Oceanographic) Data Aquisition System (ODAS) buoy, Data collection buoy | ⌑ ODAS † | 448.3 460.4 462.9 |
| 60 | | Seaplane anchorage buoy | | |
| 61 | | Buoy marking traffic separation scheme | | |
| 62 | ⚲ | Buoy marking recreation zone | | |
| 63 | Al.Oc.BuY.3s BuY | Emergency wreck marking buoy | | 461.3 463.1 466.2 |
| d | | Racing mark | ⚲ Y # | |

### Seasonal Buoys

| No. | Symbol | Description | | Ref. |
|---|---|---|---|---|
| 70 | ⚲ (priv) | Buoy privately maintained (example) | | |
| 71 | ⚲ (Apr-Oct)) | Seasonal buoy (the example shows a yellow spherical buoy on station between April and October) | # ⚲ (1.4 -15.10)    ⚲ (occas) | 460.5 |

# Q Buoys, Beacons

| Beacons | *Lighted Beacons* → P | *Features Common to Beacons and Buoys* → Q 1-11 |
| --- | --- | --- |

## General

| 80 | ⊥  ⊙ Bn | Beacon in general, characteristics unknown or chart scale too small to show | # ⊥ | 455.5 |
| --- | --- | --- | --- | --- |
| 81 | ⊥ BW | Beacon with colour, no distinctive topmark (example) | | 455.4 456 456.3 |
| 82 | ⊥ R   ⊥ BY   ⊥ BRB | Beacon with colour and topmark (examples) | † ⊥ W   ⊥ B   ⊥ R   ⊥ BW *etc.* | 455.4 456 463 463.1 |
| 83 | ⊥ BRB | Beacon on submerged rock (topmark and colours as appropriate) | # ⊥ BRB | 455.6 |
| e | | Beacon which does not conform with the IALA system | ⊥ (non-IALA) W | |

## Minor Impermanent Marks usually in Drying Areas (Lateral Mark for Minor Channel)

*Minor Pile* → F

| 90 | | ⊥ | | Stake, pole | † ↓ | 456.1 |
| --- | --- | --- | --- | --- | --- | --- |
| 91 | PORT HAND | | STARBOARD HAND | Perch, withy | † Y | 456.1 |
| | Y | | ↑ | | | |
| 92 | ‡ | | ‡ | Withy | | |
| | † | | † | | | |

## Minor Marks, usually on Land

*Landmarks* → E

| 100 | ⚬ | Cairn | † ⊙ Cairn | 456.2 |
| --- | --- | --- | --- | --- |
| 101 | ▫ Mk | Coloured or white mark (the colour may be indicated) | | 456.2 |
| 102.1 | † ⊥ RW   ⊥ | Coloured topmark (colour known or unknown) with function of a beacon | ⊥ R   ⊥ G | |
| 102.2 | † ⊥ RW   ⊥ RW ------ | Painted boards with function of leading beacons | | |

## Beacon Towers

| 110 | ⚐ R   ▮ G   ⚑ R   ▮ G   ⚑ BY   ⚑ BRB | Beacon towers without and with topmarks and colours (examples) | † ⚐ Bn Tower   † ⚑ Bn Tr *etc.* | 456.4 |
| --- | --- | --- | --- | --- |
| 111 | # ⚏ | Lattice beacon | | 456.4 |

| | | | | | |
|---|---|---|---|---|---|
| *Leading Lines, Clearing Lines* → M | | | | *Special Purpose Beacons* | |
| *Note: Topmarks and colours are shown where scale permits* | | | | | |
| 120 | 270° | | *Leading beacons (the firm line is the track to be followed)* | Bn    Bn    Ldg Bns 270° ⊹ | 458 |
| 121 | 270° | | *Beacons marking a clearing line or transit* | Bn    Bn    Lts in line 270° ⊹ | 458 |
| 122 | Measured Distance 1852m 088·5°-268·5° | | *Beacons marking measured distance with quoted bearings. The track is shown as a firm line if it is to be followed precisely* | | 458 |
| 123 | | | *Cable landing beacon (example)* | | 443.5 458 |
| 124 | Ref # | Ref | *Refuge beacon* | | 456.4 |
| 125 | | | *Firing practice area beacons* | | |
| 126 | ⊤ | | *Notice board* | NB | 456.2 |

# Q Buoys, Beacons

| 130 | IALA Maritime Buoyage System | IALA International Association of Marine Aids to Navigation and Lighthouse Authorities | NP 735 |

*Where in force, the IALA System applies to all fixed and floating marks except landfall lights, leading lights and marks, sectored lights and major floating lights.*

*The standard buoy shapes are cylindrical (can) ⌐, conical △, spherical ◔, pillar ⬙, and spar ⸬, but variations may occur, for example: minor light floats ⊏⊐*
*In the illustrations below, only the standard buoy shapes are used. In the case of fixed beacons (lit or unlit) only the shape of the topmark is of navigational significance.*

## 130.1 Lateral marks *are generally for well-defined channels. There are two international Buoyage Regions - A and B - where Lateral marks differ.*

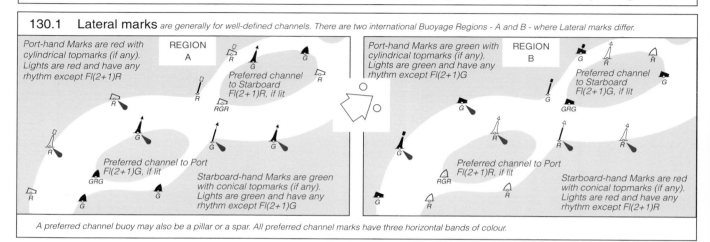

REGION A

*Port-hand Marks are red with cylindrical topmarks (if any). Lights are red and have any rhythm except Fl(2+1)R*

*Preferred channel to Starboard Fl(2+1)R, if lit*

*Preferred channel to Port Fl(2+1)G, if lit*

*Starboard-hand Marks are green with conical topmarks (if any). Lights are green and have any rhythm except Fl(2+1)G*

REGION B

*Port-hand Marks are green with cylindrical topmarks (if any). Lights are green and have any rhythm except Fl(2+1)G*

*Preferred channel to Starboard Fl(2+1)G, if lit*

*Preferred channel to Port Fl(2+1)R, if lit*

*Starboard-hand Marks are red with conical topmarks (if any). Lights are red and have any rhythm except Fl(2+1)R*

*A preferred channel buoy may also be a pillar or a spar. All preferred channel marks have three horizontal bands of colour.*

## 130.2

 *Symbol showing direction of buoyage where not obvious.*

 *Symbol showing direction of buoyage where not obvious, on multicoloured charts (red and green circles coloured as appropriate).*

## 130.3 Cardinal Marks *indicating navigable water to the named side of the marks. Cardinal marks have the same meaning in Regions A and B*

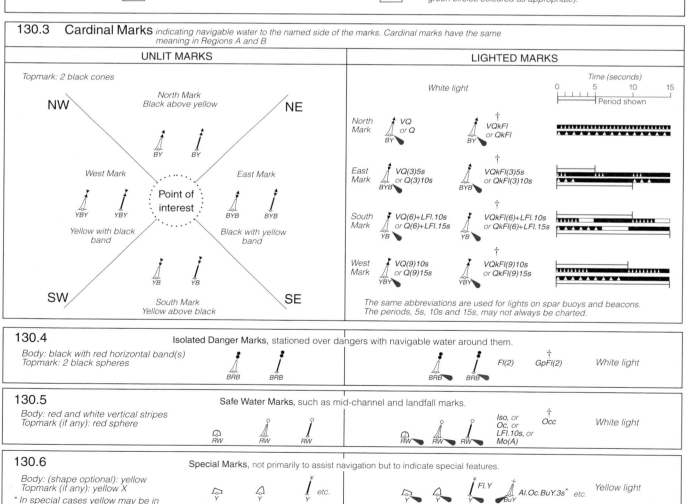

| UNLIT MARKS | LIGHTED MARKS |
|---|---|

Topmark: 2 black cones

North Mark
Black above yellow

NW    NE

West Mark

East Mark

Point of interest

*Yellow with black band*

*Black with yellow band*

SW    SE

South Mark
Yellow above black

*White light*

Time (seconds)
0  5  10  15
Period shown

| | | | |
|---|---|---|---|
| North Mark | VQ or Q (BY) | VQkFl or QkFl (BY) | |
| East Mark | VQ(3)5s or Q(3)10s (BYB) | VQkFl(3)5s or QkFl(3)10s (BYB) | |
| South Mark | VQ(6)+LFl.10s or Q(6)+LFl.15s (YB) | VQkFl(6)+LFl.10s or QkFl(6)+LFl.15s (YB) | |
| West Mark | VQ(9)10s or Q(9)15s (YBY) | VQkFl(9)10s or QkFl(9)15s (YBY) | |

*The same abbreviations are used for lights on spar buoys and beacons. The periods, 5s, 10s and 15s, may not always be charted.*

## 130.4 Isolated Danger Marks, *stationed over dangers with navigable water around them.*

*Body: black with red horizontal band(s)*
*Topmark: 2 black spheres*

BRB    BRB    BRB    BRB    Fl(2)    GpFl(2)    *White light*

## 130.5 Safe Water Marks, *such as mid-channel and landfall marks.*

*Body: red and white vertical stripes*
*Topmark (if any): red sphere*

RW    RW    RW    RW    RW    RW    Iso, or Oc, or LFl.10s, or Mo(A)    Occ    *White light*

## 130.6 Special Marks, *not primarily to assist navigation but to indicate special features.*

*Body: (shape optional): yellow*
*Topmark (if any): yellow X*

* *In special cases yellow may be in conjunction with another colour*

Y    Y    Y    etc.    Y    Y    Y    Fl.Y    Al.Oc.BuY.3s* etc.    *Yellow light*
BuY

| | | | | General |
|---|---|---|---|---|
| *Fog Detector Light* → P | *Fog Light* → P | | | |

| 1 | ((( °      ◁      ⊜ | *Position of fog signal. Type of fog signal not stated* | † Fog Sig | 451<br>451.2<br>452.8 |

| | | | | Types of Fog Signals, Abbreviations |
|---|---|---|---|---|
| 10 | Explos | *Explosive* | † Gun | 452.1 |
| 11 | Dia | *Diaphone* | | 452.2 |
| 12 | Siren | *Siren* | | 452.3 |
| 13 | Horn | *Horn (nautophone, reed, tyfon)* | † Nauto    † E.F. Horn    † Tyfon    † Reed | 452.4 |
| 14 | Bell | *Bell* | | 452.5 |
| 15 | Whis | *Whistle* | | 452.6 |
| 16 | Gong | *Gong* | | 452.7 |

| | | | | Examples of Fog Signal Descriptions |
|---|---|---|---|---|
| 20 | ((( ☆ Fl.3s70m29M<br>Siren Mo(N)60s<br>‡ | *Siren at a lighthouse, giving a long blast followed by a short one (N), repeated every 60 seconds* | | 452.3<br>453.3 |
| 21 | ((( ◁ Bell<br>‡ | *Wave-actuated bell buoy.*<br>*The provision of a legend indicating number of emissions, and sometimes the period, distinguishes automatic bell or whistle buoys from those actuated by waves* | | 452.5<br>453<br>454.1 |
| 22 | Q(6)+LFl.15s<br>Horn(1)15sWhis<br>YB<br>‡ | *Light buoy, with horn giving a single blast every 15 seconds, in conjunction with a wave-actuated whistle* | Reserve fog signals are fitted to certain buoys<br>Only those actuated by waves are charted | 452.4<br>453.1<br>454.3 |

‡ *The Fog Signal symbol (R1) is usually omitted when associated with another navigation aid (e.g. light or buoy) when a description of the signal is given*

# S  Radar, Radio, Satellite Navigation Systems

| Radar | Radar Structures Forming Landmarks → E | | Radar Surveillance Systems → M | |
|---|---|---|---|---|
| 1 | ⊙ Ra | Coast radar station providing range and bearing from station on request | | 485.1 |
| 2 | ⊙ Ramark | Ramark, radar beacon transmitting continuously | | 486.1 |
| 3.1 † | ⊙ Racon(Z) (3cm) | Radar transponder beacon, with morse identification, responding within the 3cm (X) band | † ⊙ Racon(Z) | 486.2 486.3 |
| 3.2 † | ⊙ Racon(Z) (10cm) | Radar transponder beacon, with morse identification, responding within the 10cm (S) band | | 486.3 |
| 3.3 | ⊙ Racon(Z) | Radar transponder beacon, with morse identification | † ⊙ Racon(Z) (3 & 10cm) | |
| 3.4 | Racon Obscd ⊙ Racon(P) | Radar transponder beacon with sector of obscured reception | | 486.4 |
| 3.4 | Racon(Z) ⊙ Racon(Z) | Radar transponder beacon with sector of reception | | |
| 3.5 | Racon ⊙ - - - ⊙ Racon   Racons ≠ 270° | Leading radar transponder beacons (‡ and ‡ mean "in line") | | 486.5 433.3 |
| 3.5 | Racon ☆ - - - ☆ Racon   Lts ≠ 270° / Racons ≠ 270° | Leading radar transponder beacons coincident with leading lights | | |
| 3.6 | Racon   Racon | Radar transponder beacons on floating marks (examples) | | 486.2 |
| 4 | ⅄ | Radar reflector (not usually charted on IALA System buoys and buoyant beacons) | † Ra.Refl. | 460.3 465 |
| 5 | ⅄ | Radar conspicuous feature | † Ra conspic | 485.2 |

# Radar, Radio, Satellite Navigation Systems

| | | | | | Radio |
|---|---|---|---|---|---|
| *Radio Structures Forming Landmarks* → E | | | *Radio Reporting (Calling-in or Way) Points* → M | | |
| 10 † | ⊙ Name RC | | Non-directional marine or aeromarine radiobeacon | | 480 481.1 480.1 |
| 11 | ⊙ RD — — — — — RD 269·5° † | Directional radiobeacon with bearing line | ⊙ Dir.Ro.Bn — — — — Dir.Ro.Bn 269°30′ † | | 481.2 |
| | ★ — — — ★ Lts≠270° RD 270° RD † | Directional radiobeacon coincident with leading lights | | | |
| 12 † | ⊙ RW | | Rotating pattern radiobeacon | | 481.1 |
| 13 † | ⊙ Consol | | Consol beacon | | 480 |
| 14 | ⊙ RG | | Radio direction-finding station | ⊙ Ro.D.F † | 483 |
| 15 † | ⊙ R | | Coast radio station providing QTG service | ⊙ Ro. † | 480 |
| 16 † | ⊙ Aero RC | | Aeronautical radiobeacon | | 480 |
| 17.1 | ⊙ AIS | | Automatic Identification System transmitter | | 489.1 |
| 17.2 | ⧖ AIS | ⊙ AIS | Automatic Identification System transmitters on floating marks (examples) | | 489.1 |
| 18 | ⊙ V-AIS | | Virtual aid to navigation (example). The topmark indicates the navigational purpose, see Q130. Other carriers may be used | | 489.2 |

| | | | | | Satellite Navigation Systems |
|---|---|---|---|---|---|
| 50 | WGS    WGS72    WGS84 | | World Geodetic System, 1972 or 1984 | | 201 |
| *Note:* A note may be shown to indicate the shifts of latitude and longitude, to one, two or three decimal places of a minute, depending on the scale of the chart, which should be made to satellite-derived positions (which are referred to WGS84) to relate them to the chart. | | | | | 202 |
| 51 # | ⊙ DGPS | | Station providing Differential Global Positioning System corrections | | 481.4 |

# T  Services

## Pilotage

| | | | | | |
|---|---|---|---|---|---|
| 1.1 | ⬦ | Pilot boarding place, position of pilot cruising vessel | † *Pilots* | † Pilots | |
| 1.2 | ⬦ *Name* | Pilot boarding place, position of pilot cruising vessel, with name (e.g. District, Port) | | | 491.1 491.2 |
| 1.3 | ⬦ *Note* | Pilot boarding place, position of pilot cruising vessel, with note (e.g. Tanker, Disembarkation) | | | |
| 1.4 | ⬦ *H* | Pilots transferred by helicopter | | | |
| 2 | † ■ Pilot lookout | Pilot office with Pilot lookout, Pilot lookout station | | | |
| 3 | ■ Pilots | Pilot office | | | 491.3 |
| 4 | Port Name (Pilots) | Port with pilotage service (boarding place not shown) | | | 491.4 |

## Coastguard, Rescue

| | | | | | |
|---|---|---|---|---|---|
| 10 | ■ CG   ⊙ CG   ⌐CG | Coastguard station | ■ CGFS | | 492 492.1 492.2 |
| 11 | ■ CG✦   ⊙ CG✦   ⌐CG✦ | Coastguard station with Rescue station | ■ CGFS✦ | | 493.3 |
| 12 | ✦ | Rescue station, Lifeboat station, Rocket station | † LB | | 493 493.1 |
| 13 | 🛶✦   ✦ | Lifeboat lying at a mooring | | | 493.2 |
| 14 | Ref | Refuge for shipwrecked mariners | | | 456.4 |

| | | | | | |
|---|---|---|---|---|---|
| | | Stations | | | |
| 20 | ⊙SS | Signal station in general | † Sig Sta | † Sig Stn | 494 |
| 21 | ⊙SS(INT) | Signal station showing International Port Traffic Signals | | | 495.4 |
| 22 | ⊙SS(Traffic) | Traffic signal station, Port entry and departure signals | | | 495.1 |
| 23 | ⊙SS(Port Control) | Port control signal station | | | 495.1 |
| 24 | ⊙SS(Lock) | Lock signal station | | | 495.2 |
| 25.1 | ⊙SS(Bridge) | Bridge passage signal station | | | 495.3 |
| 25.2 | †  F.  Traffic Sig | Bridge lights including traffic signals | | | |
| 26 | ⊙SS | Distress signal station | | | |
| 27 | ⊙SS | Telegraph station | | | |
| 28 | ⊙SS(Storm) | Storm signal station | † Storm Sig | † Stm. Sig. Stn. | 497.1 |
| 29 | ⊙SS(Weather) | Weather signal station, Wind signal station | | | 497.1 |
| 30 | ⊙SS(Ice) | Ice signal station | | | 497.1 |
| 31 | ⊙SS(Time) | Time signal station | | | |
| 32.1 | ‡ | Tide scale or gauge | ⊙Tide gauge | | 496.1 |
| 32.2 | ⊙Tide gauge | Automatically recording tide gauge | | | |
| 33 | ⊙SS(Tide) | Tide signal station | | | 496.2 |
| 34 | ⊙SS(Stream) | Tidal stream signal station | | | 496.3 |
| 35 | ⊙SS(Danger) | Danger signal station | | | 497.2 |
| 36 | ⊙SS(Firing) | Firing practice signal station | | | 497.2 |

# U  Small Craft (Leisure) Facilities

| Small Craft (Leisure) Facilities | Transport Features, Bridges →D Public Buildings, Cranes →F | | Pilots, Coastguard, Rescue, Signal Stations →T | |
|---|---|---|---|---|
| 1.1 | ⚓ | Boat harbour, Marina | | 320.2 |
| 1.2 | | Yacht berths without facilities | ⛵ | |
| 2 | | Visitors´ berth | Ⓥ | 323.2 |
| 3 | | Visitors´ mooring | Ⓥ † | |
| 4 | | Yacht club, Sailing club | ▶ † | 320.2 |
| 5 | | Public slipway | ◣ † | |
| 7 | | Public landing, Steps, Ladder | ↘ † | |
| 10 | | Public house, Inn | 🍺 † | |
| 11 | | Restaurant | ✕ † | |
| 17 | | Water tap | ⌐ † | |
| 18 | | Fuel station (Petrol, Diesel) | 🛢 † | |
| 19 | | Electricity | ⚡ † | |

| | | | | | |
|---|---|---|---|---|---|
| 22 | | *Laundrette* | † | ⊡ | |
| 23 | | *Public toilets* | † | **WC** | |
| 24 | | *Post box* | † | 📮 | |
| 25 | | *Public telephone* | † | ☎ | |
| 26 | | *Refuse bin* | † | 🗑 | |
| 27 | | *Public car park* | † | **P** | |
| 28 | | *Parking for boats and trailers* | † | ⛴ | |
| 29 | | *Caravan site* | † | 🚐 | |
| 30 | | *Camping site* | † | △ | |

**32**

MARINA FACILITIES

| HARBOUR / MARINA FACILITIES | Diesel | Petrol | Bottled Gas | Electricity | Holding Tank Disposal | Scrubbing Berth | Repairs | Crane/Boat Hoist | Launching Slip | Pontoon Berthing | Swinging Moorings | Chandlery | Laundrette | VHF Radio Channels | Showers | Telephone Area Code | Telephone Number | Fax Number |
|---|---|---|---|---|---|---|---|---|---|---|---|---|---|---|---|---|---|---|
| FALMOUTH - Falmouth Visitors Yacht Haven | | | | ● | | | | | | ● | ● | ● | | 12 | ● ● | +44 (0) 1326 | 312285 | 211352 |
| - Mylor Yacht Harbour | ● | ● | ● | ● | ● | ● | ● | ● | ● | ● | ● | ● | ● | 80/M | ● | +44 (0) 1326 | 372121 | 372120 |
| † HELFORD - Helford Moorings Officer | | | | | | | | | | | ● | | | - | ● ● | +44 (0) 1326 | 250749 | - |

*Marina Facilities* are no longer inserted on Admiralty charts. Users are recommended to contact the marina, or visit their website, for the latest information. Contact details are given on some Admiralty charts.

# Abbreviations of Principal Non-English Terms

Glossaries of non-English terms will be found in the volumes of Admiralty Sailing Directions.

On metric Admiralty charts, non-English terms are generally given in full wherever space and information permits. Where abbreviations are used on metric charts they accord with the following list, apart from those on charts published before 1980 where full stops are omitted. Obsolescent forms of abbreviations may also be found on these charts and on reproductions of other nations' charts.

| CURRENT FORM | OBSOLESCENT FORM(S) | TERM | ENGLISH MEANING |
|---|---|---|---|
| **ALBANIAN** | | | |
| | K | Kodër, Kodra | Hill |
| **ARABIC** | | | |
| | Djeb, Dj | Djebel | Mountain, Hill |
| Geb. | G | Gebel | Mountain, Hill |
| J. | Jab, Jl | Jabal, Jibāl, Jebel | Mountain(s), Hill(s) |
| Jaz. | Jazt | Jazīrat, Jazā'ir Jazīreh | Island(s), Peninsula |
| Jeb. | J, Jl | Jebel | Mountain, Hill |
| Jez. | Jezt | Jezīrat | Island, Peninsula |
| Kh. | K | Khawr, Khōr | Inlet, Channel |
| | Si, Si | Sidi | Tomb |
| W. | | Wād, Wādi | Valley, River, River bed |
| **CHINESE** | | | |
| Chg. | Chg | Chiang | River, Shoal, Harbour, Inlet, Channel, Sound |
| **DANISH** | | | |
| B. | | Bugt | Bay, Bight |
| Bk. | Bk | Banke | Bank |
| Fj. | Fd | Fjord | Inlet |
| Gr. | Grd, Grd, Gd | Grund | Shoal |
| H. | Hm, Hm, Hne, Hne | Holm, Holmene | Islet(s) |
| Hd. | Hd | Hoved | Headland |
| Hn. | Hn | Havn, Havnen | Harbour |
| Ll. | | Lille | Little |
| N. | | Nord, Nordre | North, Northern |
| Ø. | | Øst, Østre | East, Eastern |
| Øy. | Øne, Øne, Öne, Öne | Øyane, Øyene, Øyane, Öyene | Islands |
| Pt. | Pt | Pynt | Point |
| S. | | Sønder, Søndre | South, Southern |
| Sd. | Sd | Sund, Sundet | Sound |
| Sk. | Skr, Skr | Skær, Skjær | Rock above water |
| St. | | Stor | Great |
| V. | | Vest, Vestre | West |
| **DUTCH** | | | |
| B. | Bi | Baai | Bay |
| Bg. | Bg | Berg | Mountain |
| Bk. | Bk | Bank | Bank |
| Eil. | Eiln, Eiln | Eiland, Eilanden | Island(s) |
| G. | | Golf | Gulf |
| H. | Gt, Grt, Gt, Grt | Groot, Groote | Great |
| | | Hoek | Cape, Hook |
| Pt. | Pt | Punt | Point |
| R. | | Rivier | River |
| Rf. | Rf | Rif | Reef |
| Str. | Stn, Str, Stn | Straat, Straten | Strait(s) |
| **FINNISH** | | | |
| K. | | Kari, Kallio, Kivi | Rock, Reef |
| Lu. | | Luoto, Luodet | Rock(s) |
| Ma. | | Matala | Shoal |
| | P | Pieni, Pikku | Small |
| Sa. | Sa | Saari, Saaret | Island(s) |
| Tr. | Tr | Torni | Tower |
| **FRENCH** | | | |
| B. | Be | Baie | Bay |
| Bas. | B | Basse | Shoal |
| Bc. | Bc | Banc | Bank |
| | Bssn, Bn, Bn | Bassin | Basin |
| C. | | Cap | Cape |
| Cal. | Chal, Chen | Chenal | Channel |
| Ch. | Chap, Chape | Chapelle | Chapel |
| Chât. | Châtu, Chau | Château | Castle |

| CURRENT FORM | OBSOLESCENT FORM(S) | TERM | ENGLISH MEANING |
|---|---|---|---|
| **FRENCH** (continued) | | | |
| F. | Fl | Fleuve | Large river |
| Ft. | Ft | Fort | Fort |
| G. | | Golfe | Gulf |
| | Gd, Gd, Gde, Gde | Grand, Grande | Great |
| Ht.Fd. | H.F., Ht fd, Htfd, Ht fond | Haut-fond | Shoal |
| Î. | I, It | Île, Îles, Îlot | Island(s), Islet |
| L. | | Lac | Lake |
| | Mn, Min | Moulin | Mill |
| Mlg. | Mge, Mage, Mou | Mouillage | Anchorage |
| Mt. | Mt | Mont | Mount, Mountain |
| | N.D. | Notre Dame | Our Lady |
| P. | | Port | Port |
| | Pet, Pit, Pite, Pt | Petit, Petite | Small |
| Pit. | Pn, Pon | Piton | Peak |
| Pl. | | Plage | Beach |
| Plat. | Pla, Platu | Plateau | Tableland, Sunken flat |
| Pte. | Pte | Pointe | Point |
| Qu. | Q | Quai | Quay |
| R. | Rau, Riv, Rau | Rivière, Ruisseau | River, Stream |
| | Rav, Rne | Ravine | Ravine |
| Rf. | | Récif | Reef |
| Roc. | Re, Re, Rer, Rer | Roche, Rocher | Rock |
| S. | St, St, Ste, Ste | Saint, Sainte | Saint, Holy |
| | Som. | Sommet | Summit |
| Tr. | Tr | Tour | Tower |
| | Vi, Vx | Vieux, Vieil, Vielle | Old |
| **GAELIC** | | | |
| Bo. | | Bogha | Below water rock |
| Eil. | E, En, En | Eilean, Eileanan | Island(s), Islet(s) |
| Ru. | Ru | Rubha | Point |
| Sg. | Sgr, Sgr | Sgeir | Rock |
| **GERMAN** | | | |
| B. | | Bucht | Bay |
| Bg. | Bg | Berg | Mountain |
| Gr. | Grd, Grd, Gd | Grund | Shoal |
| Hn. | Hn | Hafen | Harbour |
| K. | | Kap | Cape |
| Rf. | Rf | Riff | Reef |
| | Schl | Schloss | Castle |
| **GREEK** | | | |
| Ág., Ag. | Áy., Ay. | Ágios, Ágia | Saint, Holy |
| Ágk. | Ang. | Agkáli | Bight, Open bay |
| Ágky. | Angir., Ang | Agkyrovólio | Anchorage |
| Ák., Ak. | | Ákra, Akrotírio | Cape |
| Kól. | Kol | Kólpos | Gulf |
| Lim. | | Limín, Liménas | Harbour |
| N. | | Nísos, Nísoi | Island(s) |
| N. | N | Nisída, Nisídes | Islet(s) |
| Ó. | O | Órmos | Bay |
| Or. | | Ormískos | Cove |
| Ór. | Or | Óros, Óroi | Mountain(s) |
| Pot. | | Potamós | River |
| | Prof | Profítis | Prophet |
| Sk. | | Skópelos, Skópeloi | Reef(s), Drying rock(s) |
| Vrach. | Vrak | Vrachonisída, Vrachonisídes | Rocky islets |
| Vrach. | Vrák | Vráchos, Vráchol | Rock(s) |
| Ýf. | Íf. | Ýfalos, Ýfaloi | Reef(s) |
| **ICELANDIC** | | | |
| Fj. | Fjr, Fdr | Fjörður | Fjord |
| Gr. | | Grunn | Shoal |

# Abbreviations of Principal Non-English Terms

## INDONESIAN and MALAY

| CURRENT FORM | OBSOLESCENT FORM(S) | TERM | ENGLISH MEANING |
|---|---|---|---|
| A. | | Air, Ajer, Ayer | *Stream* |
| B. | Bu, $B^u$ | Batu | *Rock* |
| Bat. | Btg, $B^{tg}$ | Batang | *River* |
| | Bdr, $B^{dr}$ | Bandar, Bendar | *Port* |
| | Br, $B^r$ | Besar | *Great* |
| Buk. | Bt, $B^t$ | Bukit | *Hill* |
| G. | Gg, $G^g$ | Gosong, Gosung, Gusong, Gusung | *Shoal, Reef, Islet* |
| Gun. | Gg, $G^g$ | Gunong, Gunung | *Mountain* |
| K. | Ki, $K^i$ | Kali | *River* |
| K. | Kr | Kroeng, Krueng | *River* |
| Kam. | Kg, $K^g$ | Kampong, Kampung | *Village* |
| Kar. | Kg, $K^g$ | Karang | *Coral reef, Reef* |
| Kep. | Kpn, $K^{pn}$ | Kepulauan | *Archipelago* |
| Kl. | $K^l$ | Kachil, Kechil, Ketjil, Kecil | *Small* |
| Ku. | Kla, $K^{la}$ | Kuala | *River mouth* |
| Lab. | Labn, $Lab^n$ | Labuan, Labuhan | *Anchorage, Harbour* |
| Mu. | Ma, $M^a$ | Muara | *River mouth* |
| P. | Pu, $P^u$, $P^o$ | Pulau, Pulu, Pulo | *Island* |
| Peg. | | Pegunungan | *Mountain range* |
| Pel. | Pln, $P^{ln}$ | Pelabuan, Pelabuhan | *Roadstead, Anchorage* |
| P.-P. | P.P. | Pulau-pulau | *Group of islands* |
| | Prt, $P^{rt}$ | Parit | *Stream, Canal, Ditch* |
| S. | Si, $S^i$ | Sungai, Sungei | *River* |
| Sel. | Slt, $S^{lt}$ | Selat | *Strait* |
| T. | Tg, $T^g$ | Tandjong, Tandjung, Tanjong, Tanjung, Tanjing | *Cape* |
| Tel. | Tal, Tk, $T^k$ | Taluk, Telok, Teluk | *Bay* |
| U. | Ug, $U^g$ | Udjung, Ujung | *Cape* |
| W. | | Wai | *River* |

## ITALIAN

| CURRENT FORM | OBSOLESCENT FORM(S) | TERM | ENGLISH MEANING |
|---|---|---|---|
| Anc. | | Ancoraggio | *Anchorage* |
| B. | | Baia | *Bay* |
| Banch. | Bna, $B^{na}$ | Banchina | *Quay* |
| Bco. | $B^{co}$ | Banco | *Bank* |
| C. | | Capo | *Cape* |
| Cal. | | Calata | *Wharf* |
| Can. | | Canale | *Channel* |
| Cas. | | Castello | *Castle* |
| F. | | Fiume | *River* |
| Fte. | $F^{te}$ | Forte | *Fort* |
| G. | | Golfo | *Gulf* |
| | Gde, $G^{de}$ | Grande | *Great* |
| I. | $I^a$, $I^e$ | Isola, Isole | *Island(s)* |
| I. | $I^{to}$, $I^{ti}$ | Isolotto, Isolotti | *Islet(s)* |
| L. | | Lago | *Lake* |
| Lag. | La, $L^e$ | Laguna | *Lagoon* |
| | Mda, Mad, $Mad^a$, $Mad^{na}$ | Madonna | *Our Lady* |
| Mte. | $M^{te}$ | Monte | *Mount, Mountain* |
| P. | Pto, $P^{to}$ | Porto | *Port* |
| P. | Portlo, $Port^{lo}$ | Porticciolo | *Small port* |
| Pco. | $P^{co}$ | Picco | *Peak* |
| Pog. | Pgio, $P^{gio}$ | Poggio | *Mound, Small hill* |
| Pta. | $P^{ta}$ | Punta | *Point, Summit* |
| | Pte, $P^{te}$ | Ponte | *Bridge* |
| | Pzo, $P^{zo}$ | Pizzo | *Peak* |
| S. | Sto, $S^{to}$, Sta, $S^{ta}$ | San, Santo, Santa | *Saint, Holy* |
| S. | SS, S.S. | Santi | *Saints* |
| Scog. | Sco, Sci, Sc, $Sc^i$ | Scoglio, Scogli | *Rock(s), Reef(s)* |
| Scog. | Sc, Scra | Scogliera | *Ridge of rocks, Breakwater* |
| Sec. | Se | Secca, Secche | *Shoal(s)* |
| | T, $T^{te}$ | Torrente | *Intermittent stream* |
| Tr. | Tre, $T^{re}$ | Torre | *Tower* |
| | Va, $V^{la}$ | Villa | *Villa* |

## JAPANESE

| CURRENT FORM | OBSOLESCENT FORM(S) | TERM | ENGLISH MEANING |
|---|---|---|---|
| B. | $B^a$ | Bana | *Cape, Point* |
| By. | Bi, $B^i$ | Byōchi | *Anchorage* |
| | $D^e$ | Dake | *Mountain, Hill* |
| G. | $G^a$ | Gawa | *River* |
| H. | Ha, $H^a$ | Hana | *Cape, Point* |
| Hak. | Hi, $H^i$ | Hakuchi | *Roadstead* |

## JAPANESE (continued)

| CURRENT FORM | OBSOLESCENT FORM(S) | TERM | ENGLISH MEANING |
|---|---|---|---|
| J. | $J^a$ | Jima | *Island* |
| K. | Ka, $K^a$ | Kawa | *River* |
| | Kaik, Ko, $K^o$ | Kaikyō | *Strait* |
| M. | Mki, $M^{ki}$, $M^i$ | Misaki | *Cape* |
| | Ma, $M^a$ | Mura | *Village* |
| | Mi, $M^i$ | Machi | *Town* |
| S. | Si, $S^i$ | Saki | *Cape, Point* |
| Sh. | Sa, $S^a$ | Shima | *Island* |
| | Sn, $S^n$ | San | *Mountain* |
| | So, $S^o$ | Seto | *Strait* |
| Su. | Sdo, $S^{do}$ | Suidë | *Channel* |
| | Te, $T^e$ | Take | *Hill, Mountain* |
| | Ya, $Y^a$ | Yama | *Mountain* |
| Z. | $Z^i$ | Zaki | *Cape, Point* |
| | $Z^n$ | Zan | *Mountain* |

## MALAY (see INDONESIAN)

## NORWEGIAN

| CURRENT FORM | OBSOLESCENT FORM(S) | TERM | ENGLISH MEANING |
|---|---|---|---|
| B. | B, $B^{kt}$ | Bukt, Bukta | *Bay, Bight* |
| Bg. | $B^g$ | Berg, Bierg, Bjerg | *Mountain, Hill* |
| Fd. | $F^d$, Fj | Fjord, Fjorden | *Fjord* |
| Fjel. | Fj | Fjell, Fjellet, Fjeld, Fjeldet | *Mountain* |
| Fl. | Flne, $Fl^{ne}$ | Flu, Flua, Fluen, Fluane, Fluene | *Below water rock(s)* |
| Gr. | Grne, $Gr^{ne}$ | Grunn, Grunnen, Grunnane | *Shoal(s)* |
| H. | Hm, $H^m$, Hne, $H^{ne}$ | Holm, Holmen, Holmane | *Islet(s)* |
| Hn. | $H^n$ | Hamn, Havn | *Harbour* |
| in. | $In^r$, I | Indre, Inre, Inste | *Inner* |
| L. | | Lille, Liten, Litla, Litle | *Little* |
| Lag. | La, $L^a$ | Laguna | *Lagoon* |
| N. | | Nord, Nordre | *North, Northern* |
| Ø. | Ö | Øst, Østre, Öst, Östre | *East, Eastern* |
| Od. | O | Odde, Odden | *Point* |
| Øy. | Ø, Ö, O | Øy, Øya, Öy, Öya | *Island* |
| Øy. | Øne, $Ø^{ne}$, Öne, $Ö^{ne}$ | Øyane, Øyene, Öyane, Öyene | *Islands* |
| Pt. | $P^t$ | Pynt, Pynten | *Point* |
| S. | | Syd, Søre, Søndre | *South, Southern* |
| Sd. | $S^d$ | Sund, Sundet | *Sound* |
| Sk. | Skr, $Sk^r$ | Skjær, Skjer, Skjeret | *Rock above water* |
| Sk. | Skne, $Sk^{ne}$ | Skjerane, Skjærane | *Rocks above water* |
| St. | | Stor, Stora, Store | *Great* |
| Tar. | Tn, $T^n$ | Taren | *Below water rock* |
| V. | | Vest, Vestre | *West* |
| Vag. | Vg, $V^g$ | Våg, Vågen | *Bay, Cove* |
| | Vd, $V^d$ | Vand | *Lake* |
| Vik. | Vk, $V^k$ | Vik, Vika, Viken | *Bay, Inlet* |
| | Vn, $V^n$ | Vann, Vatn | *Lake* |
| Y. | $Y^t$ | Ytre, Ytter, Yttre | *Outer* |

## PERSIAN

| CURRENT FORM | OBSOLESCENT FORM(S) | TERM | ENGLISH MEANING |
|---|---|---|---|
| B. | | Bandar | *Harbour* |
| Jab. | | Jabal | *Mountain, Hill* |
| Jaz. | Jazh, $Jaz^h$ | Jazīreh | *Island, Peninsu/a* |
| Kh. | K | Khowr | *Inlet, Channel* |
| R. | | Rūd | *River* |

## POLISH

| CURRENT FORM | OBSOLESCENT FORM(S) | TERM | ENGLISH MEANING |
|---|---|---|---|
| Jez. | | Jezioro | *Lake* |
| Kan. | | Kanal | *Channel* |
| Miel. | | Mielizna | *Shoal* |
| R. | | Rzeka | *River* |
| W. | Wys, Wa, $W^a$ | Wyspa | *Island* |
| Zat. | | Zatoka | *Gulf, Bay* |

## PORTUGUESE

| CURRENT FORM | OBSOLESCENT FORM(S) | TERM | ENGLISH MEANING |
|---|---|---|---|
| Anc. | | Ancoradouro | *Anchorage* |
| Arq. | $Arqu^o$ | Arquipélago | *Archipelago* |
| B. | | Baía | *Bay* |
| Bco. | $B^{co}$ | Banco | *Bank* |
| Bxo. | Ba, $B^{xo}$, Bxa, $B^{xa}$ | Baixo, Baixa, Baixia, Baixio | *Shoal* |
| Co. | C. | Cabo | *Cape* |

# Abbreviations of Principal Non-English Terms

## PORTUGUESE (continued)

| CURRENT FORM | OBSOLESCENT FORM(S) | TERM | ENGLISH MEANING |
|---|---|---|---|
| Can. | | Canal | Channel |
| Ens. | Ens$^a$ | Enseada | Bay, Creek |
| Est. | Est$^o$ | Esteiro | Creek, Inlet |
| Estr. | | Estreito | Strait |
| Estu. | Est, Est$^o$ | Estuario | Estuary |
| Fte. | F$^{te}$ | Forte | Fort |
| Fte. | Ftza, F$^{tza}$ | Fortaleza | Fortress |
| Fund. | | Fundeadouro | Anchorage |
| G. | | Golfo | Gulf |
| | Gde, G$^{de}$ | Grande | Great |
| I. | | Ilhéu, Ilhéus, Ilhota | Islet(s) |
| I. | | Ilha, Ilhas | Island(s) |
| L. | | Lago | Lake |
| L. | | Lagoa | Small lake, Marsh |
| La. | Le, L$^e$ | Laje | Flat-topped rock |
| Lag. | La, L$^a$ | Laguna | Lagoon |
| Mol. | Me, M$^e$ | Molhe | Mole |
| Mor. | Mo, M$^o$ | Morro | Headland, Hill |
| Mt. | M$^{te}$, Mte | Monte, Montanha | Mount, Mountain |
| NS. | Na.Sa, N$^a$S$^a$ | Nosso Senhor, Nossa Senhora | Our Lord, Our Lady |
| P. | Pto, P$^{to}$ | Porto | Port |
| Pal. | Pals, Pal$^s$ | Palheiros | Fishing village |
| Par. | Pel, P$^{el}$ | Parcel | Shoal, Reef |
| Pass. | Pas | Passagem, Passo | Passage, Pass |
| | Pco, P$^{co}$, Po | Pico | Peak |
| Pda. | P$^{da}$ | Pedra | Rock |
| | Peq | Pequeno, Pequena | Small |
| Pr. | Pa, P$^a$ | Praia | Beach |
| Pta. | P$^{ta}$ | Ponta | Point |
| Queb. | | Quebrada, Quebrado | Cut, Ravine |
| Rch. | | Riacho, Ribeira, Ribeirão | Creek, Stream, River |
| Rf. | | Recife | Reef |
| Ro. | R | Rio | River |
| Roc. | Ra, R$^a$ | Rocha, Rochedo | Rock |
| S. | Sto, S$^{to}$, Sta, S$^{ta}$ | São, Santo, Santa | Saint, Holy |
| Sa. | Sa, S$^a$, Sr | Serra, Cordilheira | Mountain range |
| | Va, V$^a$ | Vila | Town, Village, Villa |

## ROMANIAN

| CURRENT FORM | OBSOLESCENT FORM(S) | TERM | ENGLISH MEANING |
|---|---|---|---|
| A. | | Ansă, Ansa | Cove |
| B. | | Baie, Baia | Bay |
| Br. | | Braţ, Braţul, Braţu | Branch, Arm (of the sea) |
| C. | | Cap, Capul, Capu | Cape |
| Di., D-le. | | Deal, Dealul, Dealuri, Dealurile | Hill(s) |
| Fd.mic | | Fund mic | Shoal |
| I. | | Insulă, Insula | Island |
| L. | | Lac, Lacul, Lacu | Lake |
| Mt., M-ţii. | | Munte, Muntele, Munţi, Muntii | Mountain, Mounts |
| O. | | Ostrov, Ostrovul, Ostrovu | Island |
| S. | | Stîncă, Stînca | Rock |
| Sf. | | Sfînt, Sfîntu, Sfîntul, Sfînta | Saint, Holy |
| Str. | | Strîmtoare, Strîmtoarea | Pass, Strait |

## RUSSIAN

| CURRENT FORM | OBSOLESCENT FORM(S) | TERM | ENGLISH MEANING |
|---|---|---|---|
| B | | Bukhta | Bay, Inlet |
| b-ka. | Bka, B$^{ka}$, Bki, B$^{ki}$, Bk | Banka, Banki | Bank(s) |
| Bol. | | Bol'shoy, Bol'shaya, Bol'shoye | Great, Large |
| Gb. | G, Ga, G$^a$ | Guba | Gulf, Bay, Inlet |
| G. | | Gora | Mountain, Hill |
| Gav. | G | Gavan' | Harbour, Basin |
| Kam. | | Kamen' | Rock |
| M. | | Mys | Cape, Headland |
| | Mal | Malyy, Malaya, Maloye | Little |
| O. | O$^{va}$ | Ostrov, Ostrova | Island(s) |
| Oz. | | Ozero | Lake |
| P-ov. | Pol$^{ov}$, P$^{ov}$, Pol | Poluostrov | Peninsula |
| Pr. | Prv, Pr$^v$ | Proliv | Channel, Strait |
| R. | | Reka | River |
| Zal. | | Zaliv | Gulf, Bay |

## SPANISH

| CURRENT FORM | OBSOLESCENT FORM(S) | TERM | ENGLISH MEANING |
|---|---|---|---|
| A. | Arro, Arr$^o$ | Arroyo | Stream |
| Arch. | Arch$^o$ | Archipiélago | Archipelago |
| Arrf. | Arr$^e$, Arr$^{fe}$, Arr | Arrecife | Reef |
| Ba. | B$^a$ | Bahía | Bay |
| Bo. | B$^o$ | Bajo | Shoal |
| Bco. | B$^{co}$ | Banco | Bank |
| Br. | Bzo, B$^{zo}$ | Rompientes | Breakers |
| C. | | Cabo | Cape |
| Cal. | Cta | Caleta | Cove |
| Can. | | Canal | Channel |
| Cer. | Co, C$^o$ | Cerro | Hill |
| Cre. | | Cumbre, Cima | Summit |
| | Cy | Cayo | Cay, Key |
| Ens. | Ens$^a$ | Ensenada | Bay, Creek |
| Est. | Est$^o$ | Estero | Creek, Inlet |
| Estr. | | Estrecho | Strait |
| Estu. | Est, Est$^o$ | Estuario | Estuary |
| Fond. | Fond$^o$ | Fondeadero | Anchorage |
| Fte. | F$^{te}$ | Fuerte | Fort |
| G. | | Golfo | Gulf |
| | Gde, G$^{de}$ | Grande | Great |
| I. | I$^a$ | Isla, Islas | Island(s) |
| I. | I$^{te}$ | Islote, Isleta | Islet |
| L. | | Lago | Lake |
| Lag. | La, L$^a$ | Laguna | Lagoon |
| Mor. | Mo, M$^o$ | Morro | Headland, Hill |
| Mte. | M$^{te}$ | Monte | Mount, Mountain |
| Mu. | Me, M$^e$, M$^{lle}$ | Muelle | Mole |
| | Na. Sa, N$^a$S$^a$ | Nuestra Señora | Our Lady |
| P. | Pto, P$^{to}$ | Puerto | Port |
| Pco. | P$^{co}$, Po | Pico | Peak |
| Pda. | P$^{da}$ | Piedra | Rock |
| Pen. | Pen$^{la}$ | Península | Peninsula |
| | Peq | Pequeño, Pequeña | Small |
| Pl. | Pa, P$^a$ | Playa | Beach |
| Prom. | Prom$^{to}$ | Promontorio | Promontory |
| Pta. | P$^{ta}$ | Punta | Point |
| Queb. | | Quebrada | Cut, Ravine |
| R. | | Río | River |
| Rga. | | Restinga | Shoal, Sandbank |
| Roc. | Ra, R$^a$ | Roca | Rock |
| S. | Sn, S$^n$, Sto, S$^{to}$, Sta, S$^{ta}$ | San, Santo, Santa | Saint, Holy |
| Sr. | Sa, S$^a$ | Sierra | Mountain range |
| Surg. | Surgo, Surg$^o$ | Surgidero | Anchorage, Roadstead |
| Tr. | T$^{re}$ | Torre | Tower |
| | Va, V$^a$ | Villa | Villa, Small town |

## SWEDISH

| CURRENT FORM | OBSOLESCENT FORM(S) | TERM | ENGLISH MEANING |
|---|---|---|---|
| B. | | Bukt | Bay, Bight |
| Bg. | Bgt, B$^g$ | Berg, Berget | Mountain |
| | Bk, B$^k$ | Bank | Bank |
| Fj. | F$^d$ | Fjärd, Fjord | Fjord |
| | Gla, G$^{la}$ | Gamla | Old |
| Gr. | Grn, Grd, G$^{rd}$, G$^d$ | Grund | Shoal |
| H. | Hm, H$^m$ | Holme, Holmarna | Islet |
| | Hd, H$^d$ | Huvud | Headland |
| | Hn, H$^n$ | Hamn, Hamnen | Harbour |
| I. | | Inre | Inner |
| L. | | Lilla, Liten | Little, Small |
| N. | | Nord, Norra | North, Northern |
| Ö. | | Öst, Östra | East, Eastern |
| S. | | Syd, Södra | South, Southern |
| Sk. | Sk$^r$ | Skär, Skäret, Skären | Rock above water |
| St. | | Stor | Great, Large |
| V. | | Väst, Västra | West, Western |
| Y. | Y$^t$ | Yttre | Outer |

## THAI

| CURRENT FORM | OBSOLESCENT FORM(S) | TERM | ENGLISH MEANING |
|---|---|---|---|
| Kh. | | Khao | Hill, Mountain |
| L. | Lm, L$^m$ | Laem | Cape, Point |
| M.N. | | Mae Nam | River |

## TURKISH

| CURRENT FORM | OBSOLESCENT FORM(S) | TERM | ENGLISH MEANING |
|---|---|---|---|
| Ad. | | Ada, Adası | Island |
| Aşp | | Takimadalar | Archipelago |
| Adc. | Ad | Adacık | Islet |
| Boğ. | | Boğaz, Boğazı | Strait |
| Br. | Bn, Bu | Burun, Burnu | Point, Cape |
| Ç. | Ça | Çay, Çayı | Stream, River |

# Abbreviations of Principal Non-English Terms

| CURRENT FORM | OBSOLESCENT FORM(S) | TERM | ENGLISH MEANING |
|---|---|---|---|
| | | | |
| | | **TURKISH** *(continued)* | |
| | Da | Dağ, Dağı | *Mountain* |
| D. | De | Dere, Deresi | *Valley, Stream* |
| Dz. | | Deniz | *Sea* |
| G. | | Göl, Gölü | *Lake* |
| Isk. | | İskele, İskelesi | *Jetty* |
| Kf. Krf. | | Körfez, Körfezi | *Gulf* |
| Ky. | Kyl. | Kaya, Kayası | *Rock* |
| Lim. Lm. | Li | Liman, Limanı | *Harbour* |
| N. | | Nehir, Nehri, Irmak, Irmağı | *River* |
| T. | Te, Te | Tepe, Tepesi | *Hill, Peak* |
| Yad. | | Yarımada, Yarımadası | *Peninsula* |

| CURRENT FORM | OBSOLESCENT FORM(S) | TERM | ENGLISH MEANING |
|---|---|---|---|
| | | Languages of the former YUGOSLAVIA | |
| Br. | | Brdo, Brda | *Mountain(s)* |
| Gr. | | Greben, Grebeni | *Rock, Reef, Cliff, Ridge* |
| Hr. | | Hrid, Hridi | *Rock* |
| L. | | Luka | *Harbour, Port* |
| M. | | Mali, Mala, Malo, Malen | *Small* |
| O. | | Otočić, Otočići | *Islet(s)* |
| O. | | Otok, Otoci | *Island(s)* |
| Pl. | | Pličina | *Shoal* |
| Pr. | | Prolaz | *Passage* |
| S. | Sv | Sveti, Sveta, Sveto | *Saint, Holy* |
| Šk. | | Školj, Školjić | *Island, Reef* |
| U. | | Uvala, Uvalica | *Inlet* |
| V. | | Veli, Vela, Velo, Velik, Veliki, Velika, Veliko | *Great* |
| Z. | Zal | Zaliv, Zaljev, Zaton | *Gulf, Bay* |

# Abbreviations of Principal English Terms

(Note: INT abbreviations are in bold type)

| CURRENT FORM | OBSOLESCENT FORM(S) | TERM | REFERENCES |
|---|---|---|---|
| abt | ab^t | About | — |
| **Aero** | | Aeronautical | P 60, 61 |
| **AIS** | | Automatic Identification System | S 17 |
| | Al | Algae | J t |
| Al. | Alt | Alternating light | P 10.11 |
| **ALC** | | Articulated Loading Column | L 12 |
| ALL | | Admiralty List of Lights and Fog Signals | — |
| ALRS | | Admiralty List of Radio Signals | — |
| **Am** | | Amber | P 11.8 |
| Anch. | Anch^e | Anchorage | — |
| | Anct, Anc^t | Ancient | — |
| ANM | | Annual Summary of Admiralty Notices to Mariners | — |
| Annly | Ann^ly | Annually | — |
| Appr. | Apprs, Appr^s | Approaches | — |
| approx | Approx | Approximate | — |
| Apr | | April | — |
| Arch. | Archo, Arch^o | Archipelago | — |
| ASD | | Admiralty Sailing Directions | — |
| **ASL** | | Archipelagic Sea Lane | M17 |
| | Astr, Astrl, Astr^l | Astronomical | — |
| **ATBA** | | Area to be Avoided | M14, 29 |
| ATT | | Admiralty Tide Tables | — |
| Aug | | August | — |
| Aus | | Australia | — |
| Ave | Av^e | Avenue | — |
| B. | | Bay | — |
| **B** | bl, blk | Black | J af, Q 2 |
| | Ba | Basalt | J i |
| | Batt, Baty, Bat^y | Battery | E 34.3 |
| Bk. | B^k | Bank | — |
| **bk** | brk | Broken | J 33 |
| Bldg | B^ldg | Building | D 5 |
| | BM, B.M. | Bench Mark | B 23 |
| **Bn, Bns** | | Beacon(s) | M 1-2, P 4-5, Q 80-81 |
| **BnTr** | Bn Tower | Beacon Tower | P 3, Q 110 |
| **Bo** | | Boulders | J 9.2 |
| **Bol** | Boll. | Bollard | F a |
| **Br** | | Breakers | K 17 |
| | br | Brown | J ak |
| **Bu** | Bl, Bl., b | Blue | J ag, P 11.4, Q a |
| C. | | Cape | — |
| c | | Coarse | J 32 |
| ca | cal | Calcareous | J 38 |
| **CALM** | | Catenary Anchor Leg Mooring | L 16 |
| Cas | Cas. | Castle | E 34.2 |
| | Cath, Cath. | Cathedral | E 10.1 |
| **Cb** | | Cobbles | J 8 |
| **cd** | | Candela | B 54 |
| **CD** | | Chart Datum | H 1 |
| | Cemy, Cem^y | Cemetery | E 19 |
| **CG** | C.G. | Coastguard station | T 10-11 |
| **Ch** | Ch. | Church, chapel | E 10.1, E 11 |
| | ch, choc | Chocolate | J al |
| Chan. | | Channel | — |
| Chem | | Chemical | L 40 |
| | chk, Ck | Chalk | J f |
| **Chy** | Ch^y | Chimney | E 22 |
| | cin, Cn | Cinders | J n |
| **cm** | cm. | Centimetre(s) | B 43 |
| **Co** | crl | Coral | J 10, K 16 |
| | Col | Column, pillar, obelisk | E 24 |
| | conspic | Conspicuous | E 2 |
| const | constn, constr^n | Construction | F 32 |
| cov | cov. | Covers | K c |
| Cr. | | Creek | — |
| Cup | Cup. | Cupola | E 10.4 |
| **Cy** | cl | Clay | J 3 |
| | (D) | Doubtful | — |
| | d | Dark | J ao |
| Dec | | December | — |
| decrg | decr^g | Decreasing | B 64 |
| dest | destd, Dest^d | Destroyed | — |
| Det | | (see Fog Det Lt) | |
| **DG** | D. G. | Degaussing | N 25, Q 54 |
| **DGPS** | | Differential Global Positioning System | S 51 |
| | Di, di | Diatoms | J w |
| **Dia** | | Diaphone | R 11 |
| **Dir** | Dir^n | Direction | — |
| **Dir** | Dir Lt | Direction light | P 30-31 |
| Discol | Discol^d | Discoloured water | K e |
| discont | discontd, discont^d | Discontinued | — |
| dist | Dist | Distant | — |
| Dk | D^k | Dock | — |
| **dm** | dm. | Decimetre(s) | B 42 |
| **Dn, Dns** | D^n | Dolphin(s) | F 20 |
| dr | dr., Dr. | Dries | K b |
| **DW** | | Deep-water, Deep-draught | M 27, N 12.4 |
| **dwt** | | Deadweight tonnage | — |
| **DZ** | | Danger Zone | Q 50 |
| **E** | E. | East | B 10 |
| **ED** | (ED), (E.D.) | Existence doubtful | I 1 |
| **EEZ** | | Exclusive Economic Zone | N 47 |
| | E.F. Horn | Electric fog horn | R 13 |
| Ent. | Entce, Ent^ce | Entrance | — |
| | Equin^l | Equinoctial | — |
| **ESSA** | | Environmentally Sensitive Sea Area | N 22 |
| Est. | Est^y | Estuary | — |
| | Estab^t | Establishment | — |
| | ev. | Every | — |
| exper | experl, Exper^l | Experimental | — |
| **explos** | explos. | Explosive | R 10 |
| **(exting)** | (exting^d) | Extinguished | P 55 |
| f | | Fine | J 30 |
| **F** | | Fixed | P 10.1 |
| **FAD** | | Fish Aggregating Device | — |
| F Racon | | Fixed frequency radar transponder beacon | S 3.4 |
| Feb | | February | — |
| **FFL** | | Fixed and flashing light | P 10.10 |
| Fj. | Fd, F^d | Fjord | — |
| | (fish^g) | Fishing light | P 50 |
| **Fl** | fl. | Flashing | P 10.4 |
| | Fl., fl | Flood | — |
| Fla | Fm, F^m | Flare stack (at sea) | L 11 |
| | | Farm | — |
| **fm, fms** | fm, f^ms | Fathom, fathoms | B 48 |
| **Fog Det Lt** | | Fog detector light | P 62 |
| | Fog Sig. | Fog signal station | R 1 |
| | Fog W/T | Radio fog signal | — |
| **FPSO** | | Floating Production and Storage Offtake Vessel | L17 |
| | Fr, for | Foraminifera | J u |
| **FS** | F.S. | Flagstaff, Flagpole | E 27 |
| **FSO** | | Floating Storage and Offtake Vessel | L17 |
| | Ft, F^t | Fort | E 34.2 |
| **ft** | f^t | Foot, feet | B 47, P 13 |
| **G** | g | Gravel | J 6 |
| **G** | gn | Green | J ah, P 11.3, Q 2 |
| G. | | Gulf | — |
| | ga, glac | Glacial | J ac |
| | Gc | Glauconite | J p |
| | Gd, grd | Ground | J a |
| | Gl, gl | Globigerina | J v |
| | Govt Ho, Gov^t Ho | Government House | — |
| Gp. | | Group (of islands) | — |
| | GpFl, Gp.Fl. | Group-flashing | P 10.4 |
| | GpOcc, Gp.Occ. | Group-occulting | P 10.2 |
| **GPS** | | Global Positioning System | — |
| grt | | Gross Register Tonnage | — |
| | Gt, Grt, G^t, Gr^t | Great | — |
| | G.T.S. | Great Trigonometrical Survey Station (India) | — |
| | Gy, gy | Grey | J am, Q a |
| **GT** | | Gross Tonnage | — |
| h | | Hard | J 39 |
| | H, H. | Headway | D 20, D 26-27 |
| **H** | | Helicopter transfer (Pilots) | T 1.4 |
| h | h., H. | Hour | B 49 |
| **HAT** | | Highest Astronomical Tide | H 3 |
| Hd. | H^d | Headland | — |
| Hn. | H^n | Haven | — |
| Ho | | House | — |
| **(hor)** | (hor^l) | Horizontally disposed | P 15 |
| Hosp | Hospl, Hosp^l | Hospital | F 62.2 |

# Abbreviations of Principal English Terms

(Note: INT abbreviations are in bold type)

| CURRENT FORM | OBSOLESCENT FORM(S) | TERM | REFERENCES |
|---|---|---|---|
| Hr. | H$^r$ | Harbour | — |
| | Hr, H$^r$ | Higher | — |
| Hr Mr | | Harbour Master | F 60 |
| | Ht, H$^t$ | Height | — |
| HW | H.W. | High Water | H a |
| | H.W.F. & C. | High Water Full and Change | — |
| | H.W.O.S. | High Water Ordinary Springs | — |
| I. | It | Island, islet | — |
| IALA | | International Association of Lighthouse Authorities | Q 130 |
| IHO | | International Hydrographic Organization | — |
| (illum) | Illum., (lit) | Illuminated | P 63 |
| IMO | | International Maritime Organization | — |
| | in., ins. | Inch, inches | — |
| incrg | incr$^g$ | Increasing | B 65 |
| **INT** | | **International** | A 2, T 21 |
| Intens | (intens) | Intensified | P 46 |
| IQ | IntQkFl, Int.Qk.Fl. | Interrupted quick-flashing | P 10.6 |
| | (irreg.) | Irregular | — |
| | ISLW, I.S.L.W. | Indian Spring Low Water | — |
| Iso | | Isophase | P 10.3 |
| | It | Islet | — |
| ITZ | | Inshore Traffic Zone | — |
| IUQ | | Interrupted ultra quick-flashing | P 10.8 |
| IVQ | IntVQkFl, Int.V.Qk.Fl | Interrupted very quick-flashing | P 10.7 |
| Jan | | January | — |
| Jul | | July | — |
| km | km. | Kilometre(s) | B 40 |
| kn | kn. | Knot(s) | B 52, H 40-41 |
| L. | | Lake, Loch, Lough | — |
| | l | Large | J ab |
| Lag. | Lagn, Lag$^n$ | Lagoon | — |
| **LANBY** | | **Large Automatic Navigational Buoy** | P 6, Q 26 |
| **LASH** | | **Lighter Aboard Ship** | — |
| LAT | | Lowest Astronomical Tide | H 2 |
| Lat | Lat. | **Latitude** | B 1 |
| | LB, L.B. | Lifeboat station | T 12 |
| Ldg | L$^{dg}$ | **Leading** | P 20.3 |
| Le. | L$^e$ | Ledge | — |
| LFl | | Long-flashing | P 10.5 |
| | Lit, Lit. | Little | — |
| | (lit) | Floodlit | P 63 |
| LL | L.L. | List of Lights | — |
| Lndg | L$^{dg}$ | Landing place | F 17 |
| LNG | | Liquefied Natural Gas | — |
| LOA | | Length overall | — |
| LoLo | | Load-on, Load-off | — |
| Long | Long. | **Longitude** | B 2 |
| LPG | | Liquefied Petroleum Gas | — |
| | Lr, L$^r$ | Lower | P 23 |
| | L.S.S. | Lifesaving station | — |
| Lt | L$^t$, It | **Light** | J an, P 1 |
| Lts | | Lights | P 61.2 |
| LtHo | L$^t$ Ho | Lighthouse | P 1 |
| Lt V | L$^t$ V | Light-vessel | P 6 |
| | Lv, lv | Lava | J j |
| LW | L.W. | Low Water | H b |
| | L.W.F. & C. | Low Water Full and Change | — |
| | L.W.O.S. | Low Water Ordinary Springs | — |
| M | m | **Mud** | J 2 |
| M | M. | **Sea or Nautical Mile(s)** | B 45, P 14 |
| m | | Medium | J 31 |
| m | m. | **Metre(s)** | B 41, P 13 |
| | mad, Md | Madrepore | J h |
| Mag | Mag. | Magnetic | B 61 |
| | Magz, Mag$^z$ | Magazine | — |
| | man, Mn | Manganese | J o |
| Mar | | March | — |

| CURRENT FORM | OBSOLESCENT FORM(S) | TERM | REFERENCES |
|---|---|---|---|
| **MHHW** | M.H.H.W. | Mean Higher High Water | H 13 |
| **MHLW** | M.H.L.W. | Mean Higher Low Water | H 14 |
| **MHW** | | Mean High Water | H 5 |
| **MHWN** | M.H.W.N. | Mean High Water Neaps | H 11 |
| **MHWS** | M.H.W.S. | Mean High Water Springs | H 9 |
| | Mid, Mid. | Middle | |
| **min** | min., m. | **Minute(s) of time** | B 50 |
| **Mk** | | **Mark** | Q 101 |
| | Ml, ml | Marl | J c |
| **MLHW** | M.L.H.W. | Mean Lower High Water | H 15 |
| **MLLW** | M.L.L.W. | Mean Lower Low Water | H 12 |
| **MLW** | | Mean Low Water | H 4 |
| **MLWN** | M.L.W.N. | Mean Low Water Neaps | H 10 |
| **MLWS** | M.L.W.S. | Mean Low Water Springs | H 8 |
| **mm** | mm. | **Millimetre(s)** | B 44 |
| **Mo** | | **Morse code** | P 10.9, R 20 |
| **Mon** | Mont, Mon$^t$ | **Monument** | E 24 |
| | Mony, Mon$^y$ | Monastery | |
| | Ms, mus | Mussels | J r |
| **MR** | | **Marine reserve** | N 22.3 |
| **MRCC** | | **Maritime Rescue and Coordination Centre** | — |
| **MSL** | M.S.L. | Mean Sea Level | H 6 |
| Mt. | M$^t$ | Mountain, mount | — |
| Mth. | M$^{th}$ | Mouth | — |
| MTL | M.T.L. | Mean Tide Level | H c |
| **N** | N. | **North** | B 9 |
| | Nauto | Nautophone | R 13 |
| **NB** | N.B. | **Notice Board** | Q 126 |
| **NE** | N.E. | **North-east** | B 13 |
| **NM** | N.M. | Notice(s) to Mariners | — |
| | | International Nautical Mile | B 45 |
| **No** | N$^o$ | **Number** | N 12.2 |
| Nov | | November | — |
| Np | Np. | Neap Tides | H 17 |
| nrt | | Nett register tonnage | — |
| **NT** | | **Net Tonnage** | — |
| **NW** | N.W | **North-west** | B 15 |
| NZ | | New Zealand | — |
| | Obs Spot, Obsn Spot, Obs$^n$ Spot | Observation Spot | B 21 |
| Obscd | Obsc$^d$ | Obscured | P 43 |
| Obstn | Obst$^n$ | Obstruction | K 40-43, L 43 |
| | Obsy, Obs$^y$ | Observatory | — |
| Oc | Occ, Occ. | Occulting | P 10.2 |
| (occas) | (occas$^l$) | Occasional | P 50 |
| Oct | | October | — |
| OD | O.D. | Ordnance Datum | H d |
| ODAS | | Ocean Data Acquisition System | Q 58 |
| | Off, Off. | Office | — |
| Or | Or. | Orange | P 11.7, Q 3 |
| | ord. | Ordinary | — |
| | Oy, oys | Oysters | J q |
| | Oz, oz | Ooze | J b |
| P | peb | Pebbles | J 7 |
| P. | | Port | — |
| **(P)** | | **Preliminary (NM)** | — |
| **PA** | (PA), (P.A.) | **Position approximate** | B 7 |
| Pag | Pag. | Pagoda | E 14 |
| Pass. | | Passage | O 13 |
| **PD** | (PD), (P.D.) | **Position doubtful** | B 8 |
| Pen. | Penla, Pen$^{la}$ | Peninsula | — |
| Pk. | P$^k$ | Peak | — |
| | Pm, pum | Pumice | J k |
| PO | P.O. | Post Office | F 63 |
| | Po, pol | Polyzoa | J z |
| pos | posn, pos$^n$ | Position | — |
| **(priv)** | priv., (Priv.) | **Private** | P 65, Q 70 Q 70 |
| | Prod Well | Production Well | L 20 |
| prohib | Prohib$^d$ | Prohibited | — |
| proj | projd, Proj$^d$ | Projected | — |
| prom | promt, Prom$^t$ | Prominent | — |
| Prom. | Promy, Prom$^y$ | Promontory | — |
| | (prov), (prov$^l$) | Provisional | — |
| **PSSA** | | **Particularly Sensitive Sea Area** | — |
| Pt. | P$^t$ | Point | — |
| | Pt, pt | Pteropods | J y |
| **Pyl** | | **Pylon** | D 26 |

# Abbreviations of Principal English Terms

(Note: INT abbreviations are in bold type)

| CURRENT FORM | OBSOLESCENT FORM(S) | TERM | REFERENCES |
|---|---|---|---|
| Q | QkFl, Qk.Fl. | Quick-flashing | P 10.6 |
| | Q$^r$ | Quarter | — |
| | Qz, qrtz | Quartz | J g |
| R | rd | Red | J aj, P 11.2, Q 3 |
| R. | | River | — |
| R | r | Rock | J 9, K 15 |
| | R, R$^o$ | Coast Radio Station providing QTG service | S 15 |
| Ra | | Radar, Coast Radar Station | M 31-32, S 1 |
| | Ra (conspic), Ra. (conspic) | Radar conspicuous object | S 5 |
| | Ra. Refl. | Radar Reflector | Q 10-11, S 4 |
| Racon | | Radar Transponder Beacon | S 3.1-3.6 |
| | rad, Rd | Radiolaria | J x |
| Ramark | | Radar Beacon | S 2 |
| | RC | Non-directional Radio-beacon | S 10 |
| | RD, Dir.Ro.Bn | Directional Radiobeacon | S 11 |
| Rds. | R$^{ds}$ | Roads, Roadstead | O 20 |
| Ref | | Refuge | Q 124, T 14 |
| Refl | Refl. | Retroreflecting material | Q 6 |
| | Rem$^{ble}$ | Remarkable | — |
| Rep | Repd, Rep$^d$ | Reported | I 3 |
| Rf. | R$^f$ | Reef | — |
| RG | R$^o$ D.F. | Radio Direction-Finding Station | S 14 |
| Rk. | R$^k$ | Rock | — |
| (R Lts) | (Red Lts) | Air Obstruction Lights (low intensity) | P 61.2 |
| | Rly, Ry, R$^y$ | Railway | D 13 |
| | R$^o$ B$^n$ | Radiobeacon in general | S 10 |
| RoRo | Ro-Ro | Roll-on Roll-off ferry terminal | F 50 |
| | R.S. | Rocket station | — |
| Ru, (ru) | Ru. | Ruins, (ruined) | D 8, E 25.2, F 33 |
| | RW | Rotating Pattern Radiobeacon | S 12 |
| S. | St, S$^t$ | Saint | — |
| S | s | Sand | J 1 |
| S | S. | South | B 11 |
| s | sec, sec. | Second(s) of time | B 51, P 12 |
| SALM | | Single Anchor Leg Mooring | L 12 |
| SBM | | Single Buoy Mooring | L 16 |
| SC | S.C. | Sailing Club | U 4 |
| | Sc, sc | Scoriæ | J m |
| Sc | Sc. | Scanner | E 30.3 |
| Sch | Sch. | School | — |
| SD | S.D. | Sailing Directions | — |
| SD | | Sounding of doubtful depth | I 2 |
| Sd. | S$^d$ | Sound | — |
| SE | S.E. | South-east | B 14 |
| | Sem, Sem. | Semaphore | — |
| Sep | | September | — |
| sf | stf | Stiff | J 36 |
| Sh | sh | Shells | J 11 |
| Sh. | | Shoal | — |
| Si | | Silt | J 4 |
| | Sig, Sig. | Signal | R 1, T 25.2 |
| | sk, spk | Speckled | J ad |
| | sm | Small | J aa |
| SMt | SM$^t$ | Seamount | — |
| | Sn, shin | Shingle | J d |
| so | sft | Soft | J 35 |
| Sp | Sp. | Spire | E 10.3 |
| | Sp, sp | Sponge | J s |
| Sp | Sp, Spr. | Spring Tides | H 16 |
| SPM | | Single Point Mooring | L 12 |
| SS | Sig Sta, Sig Stn | Signal Station | T 20-36 |
| St | st | Stones | J 5 |
| St | St. | Street | — |
| Sta | Sta., Stn, St$^n$ | Station | D 13 |
| | Stm.Sig.Stn. | Storm Signal Station | T 28 |
| Str. | | Strait | — |
| subm | submd, Subm$^d$ | Submerged | — |
| SW | S.W. | South-west | B 16 |
| SWOPS | | Single Well Oil Production System | L c |
| sy | stk | Sticky | J 34 |

| CURRENT FORM | OBSOLESCENT FORM(S) | TERM | REFERENCES |
|---|---|---|---|
| | T, t | Tufa | J 1 |
| (T) | | Temporary (NM) | — |
| t | | Ton, tonne, tonnage | B 53, F 53 |
| | t | Elevation of top of trees | C 14 |
| Tel | Tel. | Telephone, Telegraph | G 95 |
| (temp) | (tempy), (temp$^y$) | Temporary | P 54 |
| Tr | T$^r$ | Tower | E 10.2, E 20 |
| TSS | | Traffic Separation Scheme | — |
| TV Tr | T.V. T$^r$ | Television Tower | E 28-29 |
| | (U) | Unwatched, unmanned (light) | P 53 |
| ULCC | | Ultra Large Crude Carrier | — |
| uncov | uncov. | Uncovers | K d |
| unexam | unexamd. unexam$^d$ | Unexamined | I a |
| Unintens | | Unintensified | P a |
| | Up$^r$ | Upper | P 22 |
| UQ | | Ultra quick-flashing | P 10.8 |
| UTC | | Co-ordinated Universal Time | — |
| UTM | | Universal Transverse Mercator | — |
| v | vol | Volcanic | J 37 |
| | Va, V$^a$ | Villa | — |
| Var | Var$^n$ | Variation | B 60 |
| | var | Varying | — |
| Vel | Vel. | Velocity | — |
| (vert) | (vert$^l$) | Vertically disposed | P 15 |
| Vi | | Violet | P 11.5 |
| | vis. | Visible | — |
| VLCC | | Very Large Crude Carrier | — |
| Vol. | | Volcano | — |
| VQ | VQkFl, V.Qk.Fl | Very quick-flashing | P 10.7 |
| VTS | | Vessel Traffic Service | — |
| W | W. | West | B 12 |
| W | w | White | J ae, P 11.1, Q 130.5 |
| Water Tr | Water T$^r$ | Water tower | E 21 |
| Wd | wd | Weed | J 13.1 |
| Well | | Wellhead | L 20, L 21 |
| WGS | | World Geodetic System | S 50 |
| Whf | Wh$^f$ | Wharf | F 13 |
| Whis | Whis. | Whistle | R 15 |
| Wk, Wks | W$^k$ | Wreck(s) | K 20-30 |
| | W/T | Radio (Wireless/Telegraphy) | — |
| Y | y | Yellow, amber, orange | J ai, P 11.8, Q 3 |
| YC | Y.C. | Yacht Club | U 4 |
| | y$^d$, y$^{ds}$ | Yard(s) | — |

# Index

See also Section V for Abbreviations of principal English and non-English terms, including International Abbreviations.

# Index

# Index

# Index

# NOTES

# NOTES

# NOTES